RIDGES OF SNOWDONIA

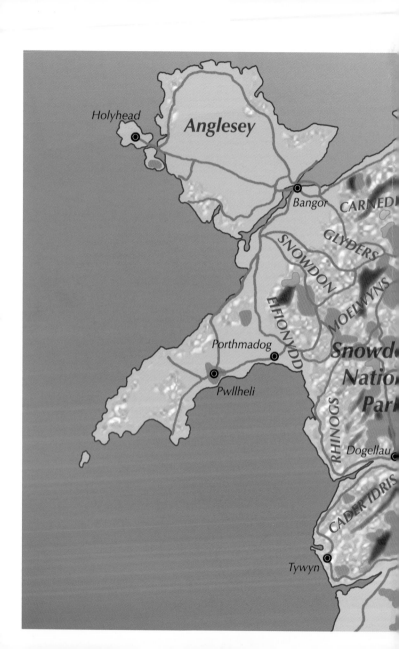

RIDGES OF SNOWDONIA

by
Steve Ashton

2 POLICE SQUARE, MILNTHORPE, CUMBRIA LA7 7PY
www.cicerone.co.uk

© Steve Ashton
First edition 1985, reprinted 1989, revised 1996
ISBN 902 363 58 1

Second edition 2002, reprinted 2005
ISBN 1 85284 350 0
A catalogue record for this book is available from the British Library

ABOUT THE AUTHOR

Steve Ashton began walking and climbing in Britain in his early teens. By the
age of 17 he had made the first ascent of a grade VI rock climb in the Italian
Dolomites. He moved from his native Lancashire to North Wales in the 1970s,
initially to work as a climbing instructor but then as a freelance writer and
photographer. He has since written ten books on hill walking and mountaineering, including the now classic *Scrambles in Snowdonia* (Cicerone Press).
For several years he was the equipment editor then humour columnist for *High
Mountain Sports* magazine, and a regular contributor of adventure travel features
to *Country Living*. He has won several awards for his writing, including the
Outdoor Writers' Guild *Award for Excellence* in 1992, 1994 and 1998.

He currently teaches playwriting at the Arden School of Theatre in
Manchester and is an actor with Cat's Eye Theatre Company.

Advice to Readers

Readers are advised that while every effort is taken by the author to ensure the accu-
racy of this guidebook, changes can occur which may affect the contents. It is
advisable to check locally on transport, accommodation, shops, etc, but even right
of way can be altered.
The publisher would welcome notes of any such changes.

CONTENTS

INTRODUCTION

This guide brings together the best ridge walks in Snowdonia. In describing them I have tried to be both readable and accurate, which explains the unusual ordering of the text. A summary of route information is given first, followed by a route description. The main routes are accompanied by a route profile and a map. The numbered points on the route profile are referred to in the route description by a small number (e.g. [1]). General chit-chat follows, and this means you have the option to glance through one or the other section according to need, and without having to plough through an unnecessary amount of verbiage.

Because the book is designed primarily for the hill-walking enthusiast, I have comandeered space traditionally reserved for introductory notes and lengthy topographical descriptions (using photographs to help compensate in this latter respect) in order to explore the hill-walking experience beyond what is normally allowed or admitted in a guide book. The resulting descriptions are progressive, to a certain extent, so that they can be read one after the other like chapters in a book.

A more serious omission in the text is that of a discussion on natural history. However, it was felt that the subject is more than adequately covered in specialised publications. One inclusion – as an appendix – is a guide to pronunciation and meaning of some Welsh words used in the main body of the guide.

For the benefit of those new to the area, or new to this style of walking, there are one or two general points and definitions worth emphasising.

RIDGE WALKING

The term is applied loosely throughout; so that in addition to following a narrow crest, a ridge walk may also be said to follow the high ground between summits, however broad it may be.

SCRAMBLING

Sections of some of these routes follow narrow exposed ridges involving rock scrambling where hands are used to assist the ascent. While even the most awkward of those included here should be within the capability of seasoned walkers, it is worth remembering that adverse conditions of any kind may dramatically increase their difficulty.

RIDGE WALKING IN WINTER

These routes – without exception – are severely affected by winter weather and its ground conditions, making great demands on winter skills and navigating ability. An ice-axe is essential (so are crampons – even if these are held in reserve); but so too is the stamina and experience to cope with what can suddenly develop into a very serious expedition. Some of the scrambling routes – Snowdon Horseshoe and Bristly Ridge among them – can be totally transformed by winter conditions, becoming potential winter climbs of some difficulty.

VARIANTS TO ROUTES

Some of these are merely alternative starts or finishes, chosen to help ease a logistical problem with transport; whereas others – full ridge walks in their own rights – are included to broaden the scope in the more popular central areas.

ACCESS

While access to all routes – as described – is presently accepted (though not guaranteed), the situation can be expected to change from time to time. This is especially true for 'sensitive' areas like Nantlle or the Arans. The Snowdonia National Park Authority have been effective in resolving recent access difficulties; but if an awkward situation should develop unexpectedly, then maintaining a diplomatic and considerate approach can only help in smoothing your passage.

DISTANCE, HEIGHTS, TIMES

All such figures are approximate. To ease compatibility with current maps, the metric figure has been given priority. Route distances and height gains take some account of terrain (e.g. zig-zag paths), so that distances and gains measured straight from the map will always give a lower figure than the one stated in the summary. Times are given for good weather and without rest stops, and they should be treated with suspicion. They have been included primarily as a measure of relative – rather than absolute – time. That is, they are indicators of the time-consuming nature of the terrain as compared with another section of the route, or with another route altogether. Compare, for instance, the times/distances given for the Snowdon Horseshoe and Carneddau Western Ridges.

MAPS

There are a number of maps available – of various sizes, scales, and surveys – dealing with the Snowdonia area. However, the following combination is recommended for conciseness:

Landranger Series: OS Sheet 115 (Snowdon), Scale 1:50,000; OS Sheet 124 (Dolgellau)

Outdoor Leisure Series: 17
Snowdonia – Snowdon & Conwy
Valley

WEATHER FORECASTS

Consult the phone book for details of
recorded weather forecasts. Daily
forecasts are also pinned at strategic
points around the park (e.g. Pen y Pass
and Ogwen Cottage). These services
are provided by the Snowdonia
National Park Authority.

ACKNOWLEDGEMENTS

I would like to thank Tony Jones,
Honorary Chairman of the Ogwen
Valley Mountain Rescue Organisation,
and Dr. Ieuan Jones, Specialist in
Accident Surgery, for help in
compiling the 'Emergency Checklists'.

I would also like to thank Del
Davies for some route suggestions, and
the staff of Plas y Brenin for the use of
their library.

A: THE CARNEDDAU

Geography lacks the subtlety to describe the Carneddau ridges: their abrupt rise, and gradual fall, in sinuous fingers towards the sea. Ridges on a grand scale; ten mile undulating strips of grass and fine stones, ideally suited to the walker going fast and far. And none of the Glyders' intricate hollows here; instead these cwms are hours long and thick with nature. But these hills are glorious only for as long as the sun shines. At other times they can be the most mind-numbing, leg-throbbing, body-chilling, toe-stubbing mountains of soil and stone this side of the Scottish border.

Rock climbing takes a back seat. There are many little cliffs dotted about the southern slopes – pleasantly secluded places for sunny afternoons – but nothing of real significance. The few big cliffs are tucked close under the north faces, secure in their shadows yet unbelittled by the vastness of their setting. Craig yr Ysfa, on the Cwm Eigiau shoulder of Carnedd Llewelyn, is the best of them. There are many hard routes here, up the vertical

The north-west ridge of Pen yr Helgi Du from Bwlch Eryl Farchog

Amphitheatre Walls so well seen from the ridge path above, but also a splendid easy one – Amphitheatre Buttress – on the opposing flank. An early start in full sunshine on this climb out of Cwm Eigiau can be an exhilarating way to begin a walk over the summits.

Winter transforms the Carneddau into a bleak and hostile wasteland. North winds blow unceasingly over the ridge crests during bad weather, so that a seemingly innocent walk becomes a struggle against time and tiredness. Fresh snow piles deep in intervening hollows, trebling approach times to the gaunt cliffs of Black Ladders and Craig yr Ysfa, now seamed with ice falls and snow gullies. A waiting game begins. Then, after the storm, when the winds have blown the ridges clear of powder, the Carneddau will offer uncomplicated winter traverses across miles of glistening uplands.

The ridge walks described in the following pages represent the Carneddau at their best: great horseshoe circuits penetrating deep into the heartland of the range and linking summit with summit along high ridge crests. Nowhere is the ridge walker's exalted position more clearly stated.

A1: CARNEDDAU: NORTHERN RIDGES

Distance/Time:
18 km (11 miles). 5 hours.

Ascent:
1000m (3300ft)

Major Summits:
Pen Llithrig y Wrach – 799m (2622ft)
Pen yr Helgi Du – 833m (2733ft)
Carnedd Llewelyn – 1064m (3485ft)
(Foel Grach – 974m (3196ft))
(Foel Fras – 942m (3092ft))
(Drum – 770m (2529ft))

Terrain:
Mostly easy walking over grass. Some sections of rocky ground.

A remote, high-level ridge walk through the heart of the Carneddau.

Ascent of Pen Llithrig y Wrach from the north on Route A1.
The ridge (partly in cloud) circles Cwm Eigiau to the summit
of Carnedd Llewelyn (back right)

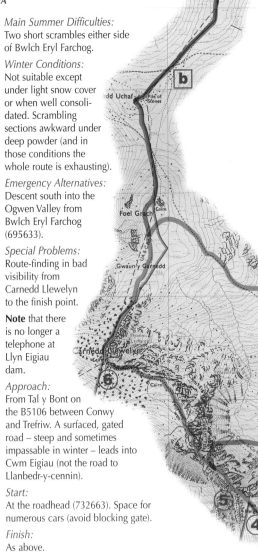

Main Summer Difficulties:
Two short scrambles either side
of Bwlch Eryl Farchog.

Winter Conditions:
Not suitable except
under light snow cover
or when well consoli-
dated. Scrambling
sections awkward under
deep powder (and in
those conditions the
whole route is exhausting).

Emergency Alternatives:
Descent south into the
Ogwen Valley from
Bwlch Eryl Farchog
(695633).

Special Problems:
Route-finding in bad
visibility from
Carnedd Llewelyn
to the finish point.

Note that there
is no longer a
telephone at
Llyn Eigiau
dam.

Approach:
From Tal y Bont on
the B5106 between Conwy
and Trefriw. A surfaced, gated
road – steep and sometimes
impassable in winter – leads into
Cwm Eigiau (not the road to
Llanbedr-y-cennin).

Start:
At the roadhead (732663). Space for
numerous cars (avoid blocking gate).

Finish:
As above.

ROUTE DESCRIPTION

A rough track leads from the parking place to Llyn Eigiau dam. Cross the outflow and take the higher track to Hafod y Rhiw.[1] Now bear up left to gain the ridge at a shoulder above its first step, continuing steeply to the first subsidiary top. An intermittent path then leads along the broad ridge before rising more steeply to the summit of Pen Llithrig y Wrach[2] (1¾ hrs).

A grass ridge leads down to Bwlch y Tri Marchog[3] and rises again – there is a good path now – to the

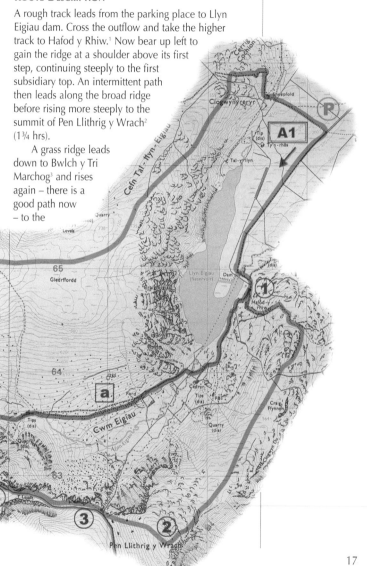

17

summit of Pen yr Helgi Du.[4] Continue along and down a rockier ridge to Bwlch Eryl Farchog[5] (where Variant (a) arrives). More scrambling up a blunt nose leads to the rim of the Craig yr Ysfa Amphitheatre. A steady rise now, up an open slope, leads to the final scree dome of Carnedd Llewelyn[6] (1½ hrs)

Circle rightwards around the head of Cwm Eigiau to descend the ridge towards Foel Grach. Before reaching that summit, and from a shallow col, bear rightwards to descend a grassy spur to a marshy plateau and signs of vehicle tracks. From the rock promonitory on the far side of the plateau, go north-east down the ridge, now reasserted, to a track leading rightwards to the roadhead (1¾ hrs).

There's something not quite right about driving north out of Snowdonia to get to the start of a walk – down the Conwy Valley, flatlands and hedgerows, coastward bound with tourists. At Tal y Bont, a bend or two before the scenery turns hopelessly flat, a single-track road strikes bravely up the hillside, serving first a small cluster of cottages, then isolated farmhouses, and finally only the whims of idle walkers eager for the hills. It ends abruptly at a junction of ways, continuing from there as a rough track fit for nothing.

This is a broad place, dominated even at a distance by a dam wall on the far side of the moor. Its sinister shape matches your every step – stone for stride. A slight detour shows it to be an empty threat: breached in its full height, the wall harnesses only more grass and more sheep. A scramble at the breach wins a brazen promenade along its elevated pavement as far as the sluice gate, where the original track is regained.

From a little way above the romantically situated Hafod y Rhiw, the circuit of ridges can now be seen almost in its entirety. Up on the left is the broad shoulder which begins the steady rise to Pen Llithrig y Wrach; while at the apparent head of Cwm Eigiau (the cwm is in fact longer and curves rightwards out of sight) stands the peak of Pen yr Helgi Du, beyond which a long ridge leads up to Carnedd Llewelyn at the true head of the cwm. The rest is hidden; although its lower arm can be seen, raised up from the far bank of the lake. All in all it seems more than a fair distance for a walk, which indeed it is.

Once on the shoulder itself, an appreciation of the scale of the undertaking is taken out of mere contemplation and planted firmly in the reality of choosing a thousand footfalls across the uncountable acres of pathless upland. And yet progress is made, height won, views gained – including an awesome glimpse down improbably angled screes towards black Llyn Cowlyd. One little jump…

The summit of Pen Llithrig y Wrach is an unpretentious place. Just a little pile of stones against which to lean a rucsac; and a small field in which to strut and flex your shoulders. There are strange views into Ogwen: of Gallt yr Ogof, unusually dominant; of Moel Siabod, a

Descending Pen Llithrig y Wrach on Route A1. The ridge passes above Craig yr Ysfa (just right of cloud) then ascends to the summit of Carnedd Llewelyn

restive whale; and of Tryfan, pinched up from the valley base like a troublesome pimple. Over there is another land, another day; but the way ahead lies east, instead, along the rim of this more immediate place, more pressing day.

The descent to Bwlch y Tri Marchog is a shameful waste when height, so recently won, is lost and must so soon be won again. In a way, Pen yr Helgi Du, this next summit, is the real beginning. Here begin tantalising glimpses towards the buttresses of Craig yr Ysfa and worries about the ridge ahead; while throughout, the looming bulk of Carnedd Llewelyn further belittles your meagre progress.

Steep and intricate though it is, the descent to Bwlch

The ridge of Route A1 crosses Bwlch Eryl Farchog then ascends to Carnedd Llewelyn

Eryl Farchog is not so bad at all. The holds are massive. It promotes confidence. Down left is the Ffynnon Llugwy reservoir, its rude access road wiggling behind like a tail on a tadpole. Perhaps here there will also be a few grunting climbers, toiling up the final slope *en route* for a day – or more likely *half* a day-on Craig yr Ysfa. There is a cairn at the col – to guide, in mist, the mystified – where winds can spill over into a different valley. Migrating insects collect here at certain times: brought up on a breeze, trapped in eddies, and no doubt wondering – just like the resting walkers – whatever to do next.

A slender green tongue of ridge ends abruptly at a rock knoll. Luckily, the knoll is an illusion of difficulty, shattered at a closer approach by the appearance of a zig-zag staircase. The path continues beyond by weaving through upright stones and nearing the dust-edged lip of Craig yr Ysfa's Amphitheatre where, on dry summer days, the rock-walled chute echoes to the urgent calls of climbers informing their partners and everyone else of their every deed and intention. Envy their situation for a moment – and they yours – because there is no time for steep rocks on *this* walk.

For such a big mountain, Carnedd Llewelyn takes quite a bit of finding on misty days (one pile of stones can look very much like another when the ground which supports them is a pile of stones itself). Carnedd Dafydd is only half an hour or so away; but the day is already long enough without tacking on any summit-bagging excursions. Yr Elen, too, is left untrodden; but it is no less shapely for it when, on the way north towards Foel Grach, its simple outline materialises beyond the ungainly dome of Carnedd Llewelyn.

There is a distant sense of return now; an inevitability of success which supercedes even the weariness of a hot afternoon and the slow drag of feet over tufted slopes. Foel Grach is near, but unnecessary; instead the slope falls away to a broad shoulder between friendly Eigiau on one side, and the unknown hollows of Dulyn and Melynllyn on the other. Only a growing awareness of scale allows you to interpret this plateau as a ridge. There, in mist, you might wander for ten minutes in any one direction without noticing a change of slope. On a clear day, though, a distant thin line of crags will betray the edge known to exist above Llyn Eigiau. Here is one last chance to feel rock and sit on summits; and at one minor top, a rare opportunity to retrace the whole walk backwards as far as its misty beginnings on the ridge of Pen Llithrig y Wrach, which is now quite near again – in distance if not in time or recollection. Enough: the lower cwm is already in view, lost in a sea of grass even the dam wall could not restrain.

A gentle valley walk followed by a steep, heathery scramble.

VARIANT (A): APPROACH THROUGH CWM EIGIAU

Distance/Time:
Reduces overall distance by 2½ km (1½ miles) and saves ½ hour.

Terrain:
An easy track, then boulders, culminating in a heather slope crossed by rough paths.

Main Summer Difficulties:
Scrambling on a headwall.

Feral ponies in Cwm Eigiau (Route A1 (a))

Winter Conditions:
A notorious slope – not recommended.

Special Problems:
Route-finding on scrambling section.

Start:
At the Eigiau dam (723649).

Finish:
Bwlch Eryl Farchog (695633) – junction with normal route.

ROUTE DESCRIPTION

A faster and scenically different approach to Carnedd Llewelyn can be made by continuing up Cwm Eigiau before striking up to the col between Pen yr Helgi du and Craig yr Ysfa.

The track from the dam sluice gates continues up Cwm Eigiau – passing numerous quarry tips – as far as a group of ruined buildings below the steep inner flank of Pen yr Helgi Du. Ahead rises the massive Craig yr Ysfa, the stone-filled slot of its Amphitheatre very obvious in the centre and emptying into a broad scree fan.

The ascent to the col on the left of the crag is not obvious. The easiest way begins first by gaining the foot of the lowest buttress left of the Amphitheatre. The path, certain then to be found, can now be followed up left-wards over heather slopes (undulating at first) until well left of the cliffs. From here it begins to wind up the slope – still trending left and crossing heathery ribs and runnels – towards the col.

VARIANT (B):
DESCENT TO ABER

A long, undulating ridge descent from Carnedd Llewelyn to the coast.

Distance/Time:
Increases overall distance by 7km (4½ miles), adding 1¾ hours.

Terrain:
Fast going along good paths and tracks.

Main Summer Difficulties:
Length.

Winter Conditions:
Tiring under deep snow.

Special Problems:
Route-finding in bad visibility.

23

Yr Elen seen from Garnedd Uchaf during the variant descent to Aber (Route A1 (b))

Start:
Carnedd Llewelyn.

Finish:
Roadhead above Aber (676716). Adequate parking.

ROUTE DESCRIPTION

Were it not for complications over transport, this pleasant descent towards the coast would be a more attractive finish than the normal way.

From Llewelyn, the route first makes its way over Foel Grach. A little beyond the summit, tucked beneath small crags on the north side, is the stone-built Foel Grach Refuge. This has the bare necessities of door, roof, and visitors book in which to enter a banal commentary on your situation.

Beyond the refuge, the ridge continues as a broad arm – grass walls, fences, summits, stones – as far as Drum, the last summit of significance. From here the ridge continues to its bitter end above the car park; or it can be quitted for the track leading down from the small reservoir tucked in the hollow down left.

A2: CARNEDDAU: SOUTHERN RIDGES

A popular ridge walk over the highest Carneddau summits.

Distance/Time:
16km (10 miles). 5¼ hours.

Ascent:
1050m (3500ft)

Major Summits:
Pen yr Ole Wen – 979m (3211ft)
Carnedd Dafydd – 1044m (3423ft)
Carnedd Llewelyn – 1064m (3485ft)
Pen yr Helgi Du – 833m (2733ft)

Terrain:
Mostly good going over grass and stony paths.

Main Summer Difficulties:
Three short scrambles: on Pen yr Ole Wen, and on either side of Bwlch Eryl Farchog.

Winter Conditions:
An excellent outing in good winter conditions. However, under deep powder the scrambling sections are awkward and the whole route tiring. Cornices can form above Cwm Lloer and above Ysgolion Duon.

A large party approaches the east ridge of Pen yr Ole Wen on Route A2

Emergency Alternatives:
Descent to Ffynnon Llugwy as for Variant (a). Descent into Cwm Llafar from Bwlch Cyfryw Drum (683637). Descent to Ffynnon Llugwy from Bwlch Eryl Farchog (695633).

Special Problems:
Route-finding on Carnedd Llewelyn in bad visibility.

Approach:
On the A5 between Capel Curig and Bethesda.

Start:
Glan Dena (668605). Parking on main road.

Finish:
As above.

ROUTE DESCRIPTION

The track from Glan Dena continues to Tal y Llyn Ogwen. Just before reaching this farm, a path goes up right – over a stile – and strikes up the hillside towards Cwm Lloer. Shortly before levelling out, it veers left and rises to meet the blunt terminating nose of the east ridge of Pen yr Ole Wen. After a short scramble up a gully cleaving this nose, the path eases and winds up through boulders and heather to the summit[1] (1½ hrs).

From the summit, a stony path circles above Cwm Lloer before rising – past a huge cairn – towards Carnedd Dafydd, where it eventually loses itself among boulders. From the summit windbreaks,[2] the path now goes due east across rocks with fine views of the Ysgolion Duon buttresses. Alternative paths further right rejoin this main one at a shallow col[3] before the steady rise over scree to the summit of Carnedd Llewelyn[4] (1½ hrs).

The path goes south-east down the summit dome, then follows open grass slopes to the rocks above Craig yr Ysfa. A short scramble leads down to Bwlch Eryl Farchog,[5] and a similar one leads out up the far side to Pen yr Helgi Du[6] (1 hr).

Descend the grass ridge of Y Braich southwards. On passing a gap in the transverse stone wall (699609), contour right then descend diagonally to cross the leat waterway at a footbridge. Follow the leat rightwards to the Ffynnon Llugwy access road and hence down to the A5.[7] Glan Dena now lies ½ hour to the west (1¾ hrs).

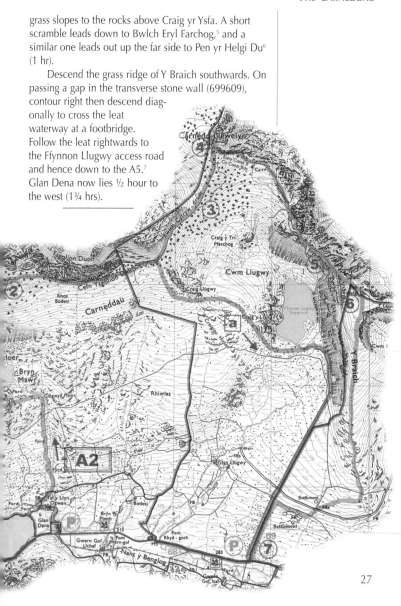

Summit of Pen yr Ole Wen

If you stand near Ogwen Cottage, facing down the valley towards Bangor and the coast, you have at each hand two very different mountain groups. On your left, the Glyders, rocky and intricate; and on your right, the Carneddau, grassy and huge. Different sides, different days.

Different, but not divorced: later that day, the views from one to the other will emphasize the contrasts and endorse the choice you made – left or right – all those hours ago. As it happens, that daunting view up the south side of Pen yr Ole Wen from Ogwen Cottage has initiated a good many more lefts than rights. This is a pity, because from Glan Dena, at the far end of Llyn Ogwen, and not much more than a mile back, is a much less tortured beginning to a day on the Carneddau.

The route up from Glan Dena is all bubbling brooks and pretty views. There is a classic picture of Y Garn – elegantly raised up beyond Llyn Ogwen, a foreground conveniently filled with well-proportioned farm buildings; and an unusual view of Tryfan, falling behind now, in an especially slender and isolated mood. But pretty views and uphill walking are together as inedible as cream and spinach. Instead the reality is one of thumbs

hooked resolutely under rucsac straps while eyes are focused – when at all – quite firmly on the ground.

Arrival of the ridge proper allows a moment to take stock. The road and its constant hum of cars, coaches and carriers is already far below (the A5 is without equal as a conveyor of tourists and frozen turkeys), and is replaced now by the clamour of seagull traffic over Ffynnon Lloer. No lesser squeal could disturb that calm. But all this is delaying matters: ahead rises a blunt nose of rock, and no promise of an easy way through. Up against it, and the shadows reveal texture; closer still and the texture reveals fissures; and then the fissures reveal holds. And now the holds themselves, large and comforting, reveal the polish of countless other grateful feet. A cool gully; a move or two; and the step is behind. Above is a twisting, heathery path; a sudden view into Cwm Lloer; and then only the great Carneddau sky.

You want to stride out, all power and progress, towards Carnedd Dafydd; but the path is bouldery, and the circling of Cwm Lloer takes longer than you'd hoped. Not that you want to get away; just that there remains a feeling of apprenticeship until Dafydd is underfoot. It

Looking back to Pen yr Ole Wen from the summit of Carnedd Dafydd on Route A2

29

The connecting ridge between Carnedd Dafydd (back right) and Carnedd Llewelyn on Route A2

comes soon enough, its summit cone like a huge collapsed cairn. There is shelter here on wild days – thanks to a cluster of S-shaped windbreaks; a brief respite in which to unravel your tongue and straighten the squint in your eyes.

Buttoned up and resolute, like ships out of port, dark shapes are seen to rise and shudder, casting off for Carnedd Llewelyn. Rounding the Black Ladders they must negotiate the peaks and troughs of petrified waves, glimpsing the horrors of the Black Pit. They gather themselves up into convoys for safety, drawn ever onwards by plastic map cases held to the fore like spinnakers in a following wind...

Thus aided, a fixed number of upward metres ought to land us on Carnedd Llewelyn. But can we be sure? On a misty day the summit is thronged by confused travellers who, like train passengers, are certain only of their final destinations. Bewildered, we clutter the platform – *Is this it? Are we here?* – while those who have the answers stride purposefully through like unapproachable station porters and disappear into the gloom. Soon we are gripped by communal panic and give up the wait. Like brave Oates we up and off into the storm, promising to return. But we never do.

If our luck is in, and if in the mist we have not inadvertently returned the way we came, or walked over a cliff, the way ahead soon begins to smooth from scree to grass. Great, delicious swathes of it are draped over the backbone of the ridge from Llewelyn to Pen yr Helgi Du. Huge, loping strides consume the slope in minutes, while a bouncing rucsac exaggerates the rate of progress like an over-enthusiastic metronome.

The best things in life, despite being free, are unfortunately almost always short-lived. This one is no exception. A stubbed toe against the first of a string of vertebrae above Craig yr Ysfa proves the point. Now begins an itty-bitty descent, picking and choosing among the bleached bones like a scavenging bird a week too late.

Suddenly it is over. Oh yes, there's still miles to go; but once planted at the col, flasks out and talk of dinner, there surfaces an overwhelming sense of return. A brief scurry down right would soon see you pounding that tarmac extravaganza down to the valley. But that is hardly a proper way to end this day. Gather yourselves up with a few scraps of willpower, instead, and attack the ridge to Helgi Du.

At this juncture, those of a cunning bent will notice a sly path contouring the slate hillside rightwards – a short cut to Y Braich. Pedants, summit baggers, and those generally short on sight and imagination will instead groan upwards on the rocky teeth of the ridge with all the doggedness of roller-coaster cars collecting potential energy to fuel their one, final, crazy lunge down Y Braich's unresisting grass.

The road walk back to Glan Dena would make for a

Carnedd Dafydd seen from the summit slopes of Carnedd Llewelyn on Route A2

31

Crossing Bwlch Eryl Farchog on Route A2. The rocky ridge ahead gives an easy scramble to the summit of Pen yr Helgi Du

cruel epilogue were the mind not already numbed by the promise of reprieve. And so it is that the sky gradually narrows and the valley sides fold up on you, one on each side – slowly, reluctantly, like a book closing shut on a bluebottle at the end of a good chapter.

A shortened circuit based on Carnedd Llewelyn.

VARIANT (A): DESCENT TO FFYNNON LLUGWY

Distance/Time:
12km (7½ miles), 4 hours, for total distance.

Terrain:
Mostly grass, with a short rock ridge. Tarmac road to finish.

Main Summer Difficulties:
A short scramble above Bwlch Eryl Farchog.

Winter Conditions:
Can be laborious in deep snow because of drifting near Ffynnon Llugwy.

Special Problems:
Route-finding in poor weather from the summit to the access road. Avoiding crags at the base of the ridge above Ffynnon Llugwy.

Start:
Parking bay on A5 at exit of access road (688603). Room for five cars only.

Finish:
As above.

ROUTE DESCRIPTION

This shorter route over Carnedd Llewelyn, though hardly comparable with the original, is a useful alternative if time is short or the weather doubtful.

Use the surfaced access road to gain leat waterway and follow it to the right to a footbridge. Cross here, bear rightwards uphill, then contour to a gap in the transverse stone wall (699609), beyond which the ridge path asserts itself.

Near the top of Y Braich, a path cuts across left to gain Bwlch Eryl Farchog directly. This avoids the extra ascent to Pen yr Helgi Du. Thereafter the route continues as for the original way, in reverse, to the summit of Carnedd Llewelyn.

The route then continues along the ridge to Bwlch Cyfryw Drum (678633) before breaking off on a broad ridge which descends south-east to Ffynnon Llygwy. Care is needed here in bad weather to avoid a band of crags above the lake. If in doubt, track southwards, returning to the shore only after reaching level ground. The access road begins on the far side of the concrete culvert, and after a short level section drops steadily down to the A5 at a calf-cramping, toe-burning angle.

VARIANT (B): PEN YR OLE WEN, SOUTH RIDGE

An uncompromisingly steep and direct route to the summit, compensated by superb views of the Glyders.

Distance/Time:
No significant differences.

Main Summer Difficulties:
Short sections of scrambling – easy but loose.

Winter Conditions:
South facing and therefore usually free of snow in the lower, more difficult sections. Best avoided under ice or deep snow.

Special Problems:
Dislodging stones onto parties below.

A cloud sea fills the Ogwen Valley below the south ridge of Pen yr Ole Wen (Route A2 (b))

Start:
Ogwen Cottage car park (649604). Overspill parking in laybys to east.

Finish:
Summit of Pen yr Ole Wen.

ROUTE DESCRIPTION

The ascent starts from the Alfred Embleton stile on the A5, on the north side of the bridge over the Afon Ogwen. There are a puzzling few moments at first – getting up or around little crags – but then only the brutal and unremitting grind up a well-worn path to the summit. Not that it is all punishment: there are wonderful views back down to the valley and across to the Glyders, especially breathtaking (if you've any left to give) in the evening or when mist fills the cwms.

A3: CARNEDDAU: WESTERN RIDGES

Gentle walking around some of the less frequented Carneddau ridges.

Distance/Time:
14km (8½ miles). 4½ hours.

Ascent:
1000m (3300ft)

Major Summits:
Carnedd Dafydd – 1044m (3423ft)
Carnedd Llewelyn – 1064m (3485ft)
Yr Elen – 961m (3153ft)

Terrain:
Grass, stony paths, and one very wet section.

Main Summer Difficulties:
Descending from Yr Elen.

Winter Conditions:
Not recommended under deep snow, when a crossing of
Cwm Llafar could be quite problematical.

Emergency Alternatives:
Descent into Cwm Llafar from Bwlch Cyfryw Drum
(683637).

Special Problems:
Navigating onto Yr Elen from Carnedd Llewelyn in bad visibility.

Approach:
From Bethesda on the A5. Turn uphill from crossroads at the
eastern town limit. Turn right at the crossroads after 1km
and find a parking place in a narrow lane, taking care not
to obstruct gates or passing places.

Start:
See Approach.

Finish:
As above.

ROUTE DESCRIPTION

At the end of the road there is a stile just right of the
waterworks gate; another at the top left corner of the field;
and a third soon after. The route then follows a stream
bed (literally!) through a culvert, and then takes a drier
path to more open terrain. A vague path parallel to the

The Cwm Llafar horseshoe seen from above Gerlan
(Route A3)

Afon Llafar leads over boggy ground, rising steadily, to a final stile, where the head of Cwm Lafar comes into view (½ hr).

A little further on, break up right to gain the ridge at a grass mound; and then follow it in its entirety to Carnedd Dafydd – first along a grass crest, then more steeply over boulders, and finally on the scree dome of the summit[1] (1½ hrs).

Circle the head of Cwm Llafar, along a rocky path above the cliffs of Ysgolion Duon, to a shallow col, Bwlch Cyfryw Drum[2] – below Carnedd Llewelyn. Continue up the scree path to the summit[3] (1 hr).

Head tentatively north of west to find the path leading to Yr Elen. It goes down to the col[4] above Llyn Caseg before rising – curving rightwards – to the flat summit.[5] Descend a blunt ridge on the west side, keeping on the left (Cwm Llafar) flank when in doubt, to a level and grassy section. Continue along this shallow ridge, passing two rock bluffs.[6] Either descend immediately into Cwm Llafar and gain the track on the far side, or continue along the shallow ridge to its end before crossing. Both are wet. Return as for the ascent (1½ hrs).

Bethesda is a sorry place. It seems always to be raining here, so that the main street twists through a hotch-potch of buildings like some grimy northern canal. Trapped by that vision, its people are wearing long coats and longer faces as they patrol the towpath. Car drivers wind up their windows and weave a way through, fearful of stopping in case they never get started again. The National Park boundary skirts the town limits and tries to look the other way.

Pinned to the hillside above Bethesda is the suburb of Gerlan; its funny little houses painted blue and pink, and so bound up with the earth that it is difficult to tell where the soil ends and their walls begin. Gerlan is the

Shangri La of North Wales, for two decades perfectly preserving its community of hippies and drop-outs. The place absorbs oddities as readily as the sea.

Gerlan has proliferated to such a degree that its uppermost house-holders are able to gaze into the sacred confines of Cwm Llafar. But, as it happens, not many of them do; and so the path up from Gerlan waterworks into Cwm Llafar remains one of the quieter places in Snowdonia.

The right-bounding ridge of the cwm begins almost straight away and yet the valley path is much too comfortable to quit so early. Lazy men's ways. Sooner or later, though, it must be abandoned for a short pull onto the neat and pathless grass of the ridge top. Over to the right now, beyond a shallow scoop in the mountainside, appears a mirage of exotic slabs. The slabs prove to be those of Carnedd y Filiast, a familiar landmark of the western end of the Glyders; and yet from here they seem much too close

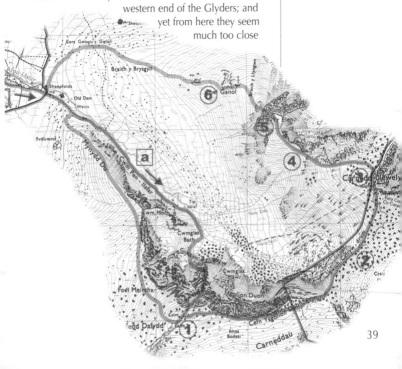

Looking back down the ascent ridge of Route A3 towards Gerlan and the Menai Straits

for that, as if the intervening Ogwen Valley had been secretly filled in during the night.

Height gained on this gentle ridge, gradually accumulated over the preceding minutes without obvious effort, suddenly translates itself into the depth of a huge bowl which is confronted at a turn in the ridge. Far below, rising up from deep within the central well, is the Llech Ddu Spur, reflecting light from its crest like a gold comb. The cliff which supports it stands subdued at its base, dark against the mottled grass of the basin floor. At the far side of the cwm, partly hidden by the spur, are ranged the dismal tiers of Ysgolion Duon – the Black Ladders; while at the nearer curve are grouped dozens of smaller cliffs, few of them explored much beyond this and other simple surveys from the rim.

There is more to do now. A steep and curving ascent around the lip – easy at first but then more awkwardly over lichenous boulders – is slow to close the gap to Carnedd Dafydd. The bowl must be even bigger than it seemed. But eventually there comes the summit cone of stones, a sense of approach, and with that a promise of views towards the main peaks of the Glyders. But Dafydd is deep within the Carneddau: the views that way are disappointing. In recompense there is a retrospect of the ridge just climbed; dramatically lit in the slant rays of late afternoon, it appears as a gigantic tail laid out by a sunning lizard.

When circling the Black Ladders on this walk, there is a tendency to keep tight to the edge; as if walkers, having earned the privilege over the preceding hours to do so, are now determined to exercise the right. In winter, sometimes, while sitting here with the rocks and a view of your ridge, ice climbers will appear from below to come and sit in the sun with you, their duvet jackets incongruous in the sudden warmth and light after the cold waits and sunless struggles below. Those passing by on gentler paths away from the edge are doubtless over from Pen yr Ole Wen and deserve none of this cama- raderie.

Beyond all rocks – from Bwlch y Cyrfyw Drum – an easy glide would have you down in the Cwm Llafar bowl, just a few boulders and bogs away from the grassed-over cart-track down to Gerlan. But the enterprise is only half done: ahead lies Llewelyn, beckoning from a bed of stones. And when Llewelyn calls, you *go.*

So large and flat is the summit area that you need to head out a good way towards Yr Elen before being sure that it is indeed the way you must go. A bit like hoisting the mainsail to see which way the wind blows. But what an appealing peak Yr Elen is – and all the more attractive for being less trodden than its bigger neighbours. It is difficult to pin down the reason for its appeal, though perhaps it is a combination of many things: the slender neck of its connecting ridge; the tiny teardrop lake sunk deep in its shadowed cwm; the view north towards other, even more remote, western ridges. On reaching the actual summit there is also an undeniable sense of satis- faction that the circling of Cwm Llafar is complete, and that now it really is downhill all the way.

Not so simple. The first downhill section is a steep ridge of economically spread scree which demands more

Looking back towards Carnedd Dafydd during the ascent to Carnedd Llewelyn on Route A3

Near the summit of Yr Elen on Route A3

concentration than any other part of the walk; and especially now when legs are tired and apt to let themselves get carried away. But the ridge turns to grass soon enough, its gentle undulations peaking here and there in rock nipples. It is at the second of these that the presence of doom, previously only a nagging doubt, sinks home with all the certainty of a dropped egg: *The Bog*. The bog is all pervading, all consuming, and all across the bottom of the valley. It separates you and the Llafar track on the far side – a not inconsiderable distance.

There is just one happy consequence: after the bog, negotiating the stream path down the culvert to the waterworks is child's play. And so back to Gerlan with a grin on your face and a smelly black tidemark somewhere up above your knees. So now who's the oddity?

An interesting ridge scramble in a wonderfully remote setting.

VARIANT (A): CRIB LEM (LLECH DDU SPUR)

Distance/Time:
No significant savings over the main route.

Terrain:
A gentle track approach to a rocky ridge.

Main Summer Difficulties:
Occasional steep scrambling sections on the ridge.

Winter Conditions:
Not recommended.

Special Problems:
Detailed route-finding on the flank of the spur.

The ridge above Llech Ddu taken by variant (a) as seen from the main ascent ridge of Route A3. The route then circles Cwm Llafar above the cliffs of Black Ladders seen in the background

Start:
As for the normal route.

Finish:
Summit of Carnedd Dafydd.

ROUTE DESCRIPTION

This is an exciting way to start the walk for those with some previous experience of scrambling. Technical difficulties are no greater than those encountered on Bristly Ridge; but there are the added problems of lichenous rock and loose holds. Detailed route-finding is also more difficult because the spur is climbed much less often.

Instead of breaking off right from the valley approach, continue along it as far as a group of huge boulders below the cliff of Llech Ddu (666638). The cliff bars direct entry to the spur, and so a way to avoid it must be found. In fact it can be flanked completely by ascending into the cwm to its right almost to the level of the base of the gully splitting Craig y Cwmglas Bach, at which point a ramp of grass and stones slanting diagonally left between bands of rock will be revealed. This leads without complication to a bilberry shoulder on the spur above Llech Ddu.

The spur itself, broad at first, soon narrows to give interesting scrambling over short obstacles and along grass arêtes. All too soon the crest falls back and merges into the barren summit dome.

B: THE GLYDERS

The Glyders are friendly. With or without cause, it would be hard to find a harsh word to say about them. But let's be ruthless for a moment. The term *Glyders* is normally spoken with such generous implication, usually accompanied by a wide sweep of the arm, that a newcomer might wonder if the promise of 'A day on the Glyders' involves an enormous traverse across endless tracts of rugged mountainside. In fact 'the Glyders' is something rather less. Think of it this way: on the map, place a compass point on the A5, a little to the east of Ogwen Cottage, and describe a semi-circle with the radius set at Glyder Fawr summit (you can also do this 'in the field' by letting your eyes sweep the skyline – the result is much the same). That semi-circle is 'the Glyders'. And yet if that small area is able to conjure up so mighty an image, then it must surely have something very special to offer.

It has: ridge scrambles, mountain rock climbs, ice routes – the lot. Add to this its accessibility and rich history, and you have an unbeatable recipe for popularity. But what of the rest? Walking those parts of the range which fall outside the semi-circle is to experience a loneliness like being outside a football stadium with a game in progress, the excitement and the cheers spilling over into the streets. *What is going on in there? Am I missing something?* No wonder most days on the Glyders – however independent in the beginning – eventually wind up on one or other of the main summits. Nothing wrong in that, because these moody summits have a rare chameleon quality not often found on any of the Snowdon or Carneddau tops. In other words, they are among the few summits worth saving lunch for.

B1: GLYDERS:
NORTHERN RIDGES

A series of rock ridges, logically combined to give a magnificent scrambling day.

Distance/Time:
8km (5 miles). 4½ hours.

Ascent:
900m (3000ft)

Major Summits:
Tryfan – 917m (3010ft)
Glyder Fach – 994 m (3262ft)
(Glyder Fawr – 999m (3279ft))
(Y Garn – 946m (3104ft))

Terrain:
Rock ridges and stony paths. Some boggy ground.

Main Summer Difficulties:
Ascent of Tryfan, descent to Bwlch Tryfan, ascent of Bristly Ridge, and descent of upper part of the Gribin.

Winter Conditions:
A winter climb, not a scramble.

Emergency Alternatives:
Descent to Bochlwyd from Bwlch Tryfan (as for Variant (a) in reverse). Scree couloir on east side of Bristly Ridge (avoids scramble).

Special Problems:
Detailed route-finding on each scrambling section. Route-finding in mist over Glyder Fach summit area.

Approach:
Along A5 between Capel Curig and Bethesda.

Start:
Layby below Milestone Buttress (663603). Adequate parking.

Finish:
As above.

ROUTE DESCRIPTION

Go over the stile at the layby and follow the high wall which runs up to the base of the Milestone Buttress. Just before reaching the cliffs, break off left and zig-zag up the shoulder to where a view opens out to the east, showing the obvious smooth slab of Little Tryfan far

The first section of Route B1 approximately follows the skyline as it traverses Tryfan (right) then ascends Bristly Ridge (left) to the summit of Glyder Fach below. (This point can also be reached by starting from Gwern Gof Uchaf.) Above a scree cone is a multitude of paths, each of which tackles the blunt north ridge with greater or lesser effect. From a level section above, the Cannon may be found over on the right; while the route continues up left to a rock pavement and some more easy scrambling. After another level section, the ridge gathers itself into a narrow rib of rock – tricky but on sound rock – followed by a short descent to a notch. A short scramble out of this gains first the North Summit and then – gained easily – the Main Summit, positively identified in mist by the unique standing stones of Adam and Eve[1] (1¾ hrs).

The best way of descending the South Ridge is to keep as near to the crest as practical – over the South and Far South summits – and so directly down to Bwlch Tryfan[2] (½ hr).

The start of Bristly Ridge is not obvious. The most reliable way is to follow the stone wall up to the base of the crags; then go about 10m right, entering a little gully.

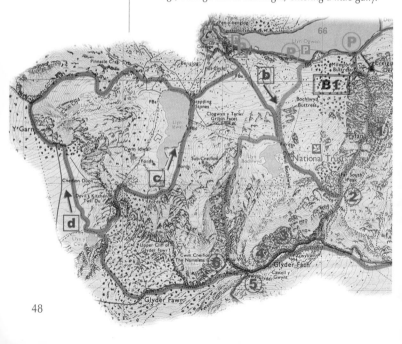

Go up the gully and cross a *garden wall* leftwards at its top. Above is the *sinister gully*. Where it steepens uncomfortably, move left out onto a rib, and then back right a little higher to reach easy ground. Beyond is a shoulder formed by rock slabs. The ridge narrows above. After crossing one small pinnacle, there is a longer ascent to the top of a minor summit. Ahead now is Great Pinnacle Gap. Descend almost directly into the gap, then up a short wall, just right of the slender Great Pinnacle, to a recess behind it. Now go through a gap between the squat pinnacle and the main body of the ridge to easy ground.[3] A final, level ridge crest leads onto the summit plateau. The path now bears right (the Cantilever – an unusual and much photographed perch – is over on the left) to a pile of huge blocks forming the summit[4] (1 hr).

Continuing on the same line, the path leads to the shapely crag of Castell y Gwynt, through which a direct way can be found (or avoided well down on the left). From a shallow col beyond,[5] ignore the well-worn path to Glyder Fawr and ascend directly to the bulky prominence marking the top of the Gribin.[6] The upper section of the Gribin is quite tricky in descent, but difficulties soon ease where the path leads into a grass field. The path is followed along the ridge until it branches off right to gain the north shore of Llyn Bochlwyd (¾ hr).

The path descending near the stream out of Bochlwyd can be followed all the way to Ogwen Cottage; however there is a more convenient

49

*Summit of Tryfan;
Gribin Ridge in
background*

return: after the steep part of the descent, bear right (passing below the smooth crag of Bochlwyd Buttress) to find a way down and across boggy ground eastwards. A final steep descent down a rock-studded rib leads to a parking bay on the A5, not far from the starting point (½ hr).

Tryfan is so commonplace an objective that there is a danger of it being undervalued – 'Tryfan, only Tryfan?' – whereas in fact there is nothing 'only' about it at all. Fancying itself a cut above the rest, it juts proudly into the valley with its foot thrust out, ready to trip you up should you – like George Borrow – try to pass it by. 'Look at this then,' it says, rolling up the veils of mist to reveal its naked north ridge. And you do; because that bristling leg is where the route begins.

At first the ridge is broad and disappointing. What seemed so slim and elegant from the road is, at close approach, nothing but a fudge of scree and boulders. Apart from a stout wall, the only coherent form among the jumble is a scab of coagulated rock called the Milestone Buttress – a crag over which dozens of climbers

*On the traverse of
Tryfan between central
and south summits*

daily crawl like a mess of ants. At the shoulder, too, there
is little evidence of promised ridges. Only the apparent
transformation of roads to ribbons is indication of real
progress.

Not that the terrain is especially easy. There must be
a dozen ways above the shoulder, yet no matter which
one is chosen it proves to be unnecessarily obstructive.
Awkward little steps with scree finishes – none individu-
ally difficult, but having the cumulative effect of
belligerency. The Cannon goes by, tucked down right
beneath a rock wall and missed by many (but not by
others who pose shamelessly on its barrel for photographs); and *still* the ridge will not get itself together.

Ah, but when it does you can guarantee to find those
who did the most complaining dithering about the flanks
and trying to avoid the issue (the issue being the smooth-
looking cone of rock). It does look a problem... But not
on sunny days. Not when every wrinkle proves to be a
large and solid edge conforming to a ladder-like
frequency of holds. Scrambling? This is it.

A tricky descent to a boulder-filled notch is not so
predictable. When wind-driven snow transforms the rock

to green-slimed dragon scales (when perhaps it really would have been better to sneak around the side), all the mountain's hostility seems to be focused at this one place; so that the cold becomes doubly cold, and the very next step you take is the only one that matters.

And suddenly the summit: an elevated bandstand where walkers and climbers and dogs gather to listen to ghostly music and to watch the seagulls swirl in wind-blown spirals like the litter of past performances. A ballet is being danced on the two great monoliths of Adam and Eve. On the northern stone (no-one knows which is Adam and which is Eve, and there are few clinical clues disclosed by their innocent anatomies), there pirouettes a

Respite on Tryfan's North Ridge (Route B1)

person evidently suffering from the nervous excitement of anticipating a spring across the gap to the southern stone. He (for invariably it is a *he*) is obliged by honour to consummate his boast, and seems about to do so at any second. But the seconds pass, become minutes, and *still* he hesitates. By this time his friends have grown tired of offering words of encouragement, and a couple of them have even wandered to the far side of the jump to see what would be the outcome of a miscalculation on the part of their companion. They shake their heads. Suddenly he takes to the air and is across. *I did it! I did it! Did you see!* But no-one had; and were it not for the indisputable evidence of him now being on a different

Notch below the north summit of Tryfan (Route B1). Note the rock climbers on the North Butress below

53

rock, his claim might well have been refuted. 'Nothing to it', he says, lowering himself down to his sandwiches.

Time passes. A polished neck leads down onto the rocks of South Summit, beyond which a snakes-and-ladders scramble down rock terraces leads to the walled col below the Glyders. Attention is attracted first by the winking eye of Llyn Bochlwyd, shimmering from its sunken hollow, but is soon drawn back to the stone grey crags of Glyder Fach ahead, because among them is the line of Bristly Ridge, looming like the sudden prow of a ship in a sea fog.

The wall points the way: up into a clammy gully where it feels as if the retaining wall is about to fold over you like pastry on a pie. The epitome of anti-ridge. After

Descending into Great Pinnacle Gap on Bristly Ridge (Route B1)

that, the pinnacles of the ridge proper are especially welcome – leastways as far as the Great Pinnacle Gap. Here, while peering longingly across the void at the continuation ridge, there is a weird sensation of being marooned on a parting iceflow – Nanook and sledge on far side, you and polar bear on this. Resource and necessity finds a way: down a miniature helter-skelter; over a garden wall; along a catwalk; and finally through a turnstile to easy ground. You've cracked it. It now remains only for you to promenade along the raised pavement of rock slabs so everyone will know that *you* came up by Bristly Ridge.

So this is Glyder Fach. If there is such a thing in hell as a play park then I expect it will look something like this. A place where, instead of soft grass, there is only unyielding rock to cushion your misadventures; where the rocking horse has turned to stone and will not move – not even under the combined weight of an entire year's worth of Hebden Bridge Secondary School and their not inconsiderable lunch; and where the climbing frame is undermined by chasms so deep that little kids can disappear for hours at a time. People of all ages come to play here in their hundreds: to fall from slides onto blades of rock; to twist their ankles and drop down holes; and maybe even to get eaten by goblins, some of them. And then they'll wander over to Castell y Gwynt where the *real* trouble starts...

Not really; but whichever way you go – around its perimeter or over the drawbridge – the flatlands beyond Castell y Gwynt are a paradise for feet. All the more a pity, then, to abandon them for a rocky plunge down the Gribin. Having once switched off, switching back on for this few hundred feet of rock is a bind. But it doesn't last long; a short scramble, a few scree slopes, and then only a delightful stroll along its gently dipping crest. The inner view is of now familiar Bochlwyd, its lake half in shade and the cliffs above taking on a reddish hue in the afternoon sun. The outward view is of Idwal, Ogwen, and as much of the Carneddau as the heat haze permits.

The ridge fizzles out at Bochlwyd lakeside. Here there is a bog; perhaps a tent or two; people eating

On the descent of the Gribin Ridge (Route B1)

dinner; and midges eating you. Nothing for it, then, but to mimic the stream cascade into Ogwen – stumbling and grumbling (but also bubbling a little) down the steep hillside. There is a shortcut under Bochlwyd Buttress (evening climbers slow in the sun), and then a steep zigzag down onto the road. And with that, when it's all over, there is the slow sinking feeling that the day has been so very much better than you ever gave it credit for.

VARIANT (A): BRAICH Y DDEUGWM APPROACH

A pleasant and unfrequented ridge leading more directly onto Glyder Fach. Unusual views of Tryfan.

Distance/Time:
Quicker than the normal way, despite being slightly longer.

Terrain:
Mostly grass (one boggy section), and some optional rock sections.

Main Summer Difficulties:
Avoidable short scrambles on the lower part.

Winter Conditions:
One of the more reliable winter routes onto or off the Glyders.

Special Problems:
Electric fence! Bogs near Llyn y Caseg Fraith.

Start:
Gwern y Gof Isaf (685601). Adequate parking (small fee).

Finish:
Summit of Glyder Fach.

ROUTE DESCRIPTION

There is a stile west of the farmhouse, and although the usual way is to go over a second stile almost immediately on the left, a much more interesting and scenic way is to follow the intermittently rocky ridge crest (go down left to a stile at an electric fence). The ridge leads naturally onto a grassy plateau at the little lake. Glyder Fach is due west from here– across bogs and then up stony paths.

> **VARIANT (B):**
> **BOCHLWYD APPROACH**

A direct, varied approach to Bristly Ridge.

Distance/Time:
A little shorter than the normal way and very much quicker. Reduces overall time by 1¼ hours.

Terrain:
Well-worn paths.

Main Summer Difficulties:
Steep walking up to Llyn Bochlwyd.

Winter Conditions:
Not seriously affected by most conditions.

Start:
Ogwen Cottage (649603), or layby on A5 (659602). Adequate parking.

Finish:
Bwlch Tryfan (662587).

ROUTE DESCRIPTION

Bear left at the first sharp curve on the Idwal path, crossing boggy ground – stepping-stones – to the start of a steep rise up the badly eroded slope to Cwm Bochlwyd (or reach this point from the layby). At Bochlwyd, the path levels and then rises gradually to Bwlch Tryfan at a junction with the normal route.

Extends the normal route over Glyder Fawr.

VARIANT (C):
KITCHEN DESCENT

Distance/Time:
Adds 3km (2 miles) and more than 1 hour.

Terrain:
Rock and scree paths. Boulders.

Main Summer Difficulties:
Descending lower part of Kitchen ramp.

Winter Conditions:
The Kitchen path can be extremely insecure in descent under snow, and is even worse when iced. Not recommended.

Special Problems:
Note that the Kitchen path does *not* take the wide vertical cleft in the centre of the cliffs. Although it is possible to scramble a little way into this unique chasm – and even a little way down from the top – the actual path takes a leftward diagonal line on the left.

Start:
Castell y Gwynt (654582).

Finish:
Ogwen Cottage (649603).

ROUTE DESCRIPTION

From Castell y Gwynt, ignore the detour needed to reach the top of the Gribin and follow the main path instead, across the hillside to the left. After circling the lip of Cwm Cneifion, this leads directly to the strange rock piles of Glyder Fawr summit.

The descent to Llyn y Cŵn – a scree run without the scree – is not easy to follow in the mist, despite (or perhaps because of) dozens of cairns spread about the place. Begin by descending the shoulder south-west from the summit for about 200m before turning north-west. From the lake the Kitchen path is found to the north-east by following a small, stone-based canyon. At the start of the descent, the path follows a very broad ramp. This narrows near its base, and there is a short section of scrambling to reach the foot of the Devil's Kitchen itself. Now go down over awkward boulders to find the start of a well-made path which slants down towards the east side of Llyn Idwal, passing below the impressive sweep of Idwal Slabs. It remains then only to hobble along the Idwal Path to Ogwen Cottage.

VARIANT (D):
Y GARN DESCENT

Distance/Time:
Adds 4km (2½ miles) and 1½ hours.

Terrain:
Well-worn paths.

Main Summer Difficulties:
Very easy scrambling down Y Garn north-east ridge.

Winter Conditions:
Axe and crampons required to descend ridge in full winter conditions, when it can be very good.

Start:
Castell y Gwynt (654582).

Finish:
Ogwen Cottage (649603).

A popular and worthwhile extension to the normal route over two major summits.

The ascent of Y Garn on variant B1(d). Tryfan (left) and Glyder Fach in the background

Route Description

Follow Variant (c) as far as Llyn y Cŵn (638585); then continue up to Y Garn by a good path – a tiring slope after a long day. The north-east ridge descent (not to be confused with a ridge starting on the Llyn y Cŵn side) is reached by first descending slightly north-west – to a cairn – from where the ridge descends as a narrow crest to a broader and more level section. The path swings yet further east where the ridge broadens again, zig-zagging down a blunt shoulder. Now head for the north shore of Llyn Idwal, where a bridge across the outflow leads onto the main Idwal Path to Ogwen Cottage.

B2 GLYDERS: MAIN TRAVERSE

A long and varied walk offering unrivalled views of this and neighbouring ranges.

Distance/Time:
20km (12½ miles). 7 hours.

Ascent:
1500m (5000ft)

Major Summits
Carnedd y Filiast – 821m (2695ft)
Mynydd Perfedd – 812m (2665ft)
Foel Goch – 831m (2727ft)
Y Garn – 946m (3104ft)
Glyder Fawr – 999m (3279ft)
Glyder Fach – 994m (3262ft)
Gallt yr Ogof – 762m (2499ft)

Terrain:
Mainly grass, but with a long central section over stones and scree. Some boggy ground.

Main Summer Difficulties:
Length.

Winter Conditions:
No particular difficulties, but length is a problem.

Emergency Alternatives:
Numerous descents from the ridge (see Section B1).

Special Problems:
Problems with route-finding in bad visibility apply to the full length of the ridge. Possible trespass problems at Penrhyn Quarry (if in doubt, start from Dol Awen – 631648).

Approach:
Along A5 between Capel Curig and Bethesda.

Start:
Layby at Ogwen Bank (627654). Adequate parking.

Finish:
Capel Curig (721582).

ROUTE DESCRIPTION

From the layby, go down the track and over the bridge. Turn right to gain and follow an incline leading back up left. Cross slate spoil on the right to reach the main quarry track, which winds up to the highest workings.

Looking down the Ogwen Valley from the ridge between
Foel Goch and Y Garn on Route B2

Tremendous views into the quarry. From the top of the road, gain the end of the ridge at a cairn (1 hour).

A narrow path goes along the crest to the first major summit – the rocky top of Carnedd y Filiast.[1] Continue over Mynydd Perfedd,[2] dropping gently over grass to the col below Foel Goch.[3] A sharp ascent of this is rewarded by superb views in all directions[4] (1 hour).

The ridge fall gently at first,[5] but then rises sharply again – over scree – to the rock summit of Y Garn.[6] Another fine viewpoint (1½ hr).

A good path takes you quickly down to Llyn y Cŵn,[7] from where an interminable grind up scree paths wins Glyder Fawr[8] – the highest point of the traverse (1½ hrs).

Rock-covered paths, then a soil rut, lead to a shallow col below Castell y Gwynt.[9] Find a way through the pinnacles (or dodge them down right) and continue over boulder pavements to Glyder Fach[10] (½ hr).

Continue due east, first on rock then dropping down to grass slopes and the bogs near Llyn y Caseg Fraith.[11] The path becomes less distinct, rising and falling over gentle hills, until it loses itself among small crags at the end of the ridge. Find a way down to emerge on a track at Gelli (720585) (2½ hrs).

It takes about fifteen minutes to drive from Capel Curig to Bethesda. The walk along the skyline ridge which parallels that journey takes somewhat longer. It is a big outing, set more in the mould of a Carneddau traverse than a Glyders ridge; and so if it's length you're after, this is the one.

The day begins early and starts with a shock: Penrhyn Slate Quarry. It would have been possible to bypass this leprous extremity of the ridge,

*Looking back towards
Castell y Gwynt and
Glyder Fawr from
Glyder Fach on
Route B2*

were it not for that curious human condition which compels us to inspect exposed guts. The mountain has been half eaten away. In the pit of its dull grey sore, the mammoth trucks can be seen wriggling into the piles of spoil like maggots in the pus of an infected limb. But it seems the earth is rotten to the core: they'll never find another green hill, no matter how deep they dig.

So extensive are these workings that is takes no time at all to get from the top of the quarry road to the tip of the first hill on the ridge. There are no footpaths here – only the trailmarks of preceding itchy feet that also found themselves here after long and conventional upbringings on the main peaks of the Glyders. This is connoisseur's territory.

Carnedd y Filiast is not so threatened. At its summit there is opportunity for a more dispassionate appraisal of

*A precarious moment
on the iced finger of
the Cantilever on
Glyder Fach
(Route B2)*

the surroundings: of the quarry behind, growing quiet and distant; of the road below, not yet alive with the day's traffic; and of the Marchlyn Mawr dam, a *fait accompli* against the inner sanctum of Elidir Fawr. Smugly safe, frozen in a moment of time, the creeping threat stays frozen too. But don't breathe, don't dare move. Move and the threat resumes: surfer on a wave; rabbit in a corn-field. Too late: wave breaks; scythes cut. Better keep going.

From a small promontory there is a view of the Filiast slabs – a thousand foot expanse of rock, studiously ignored (for reasons known only to themselves) by generations of rock climbers. These slabs typify the contrasts that exist throughout between north and south sides of the ridge. On one flank are deeply penetrating cwms, each walled by crags and separated by jagged ridges; and on the other, rolling grasslands grazed at leisure by indifferent sheep. Most people out today will be committed to just one or the other. Here, though, you may tread the fine line between and sample both.

Elidir Fawr seems quite close in this light: a shapely head held slightly aloof by its slender grass neck. But

there is no time for detours today, not even on that scale; and especially now that Tryfan has appeared some awesome distance away, a reminder of the task ahead. Not that this urgency need deter an ascent to Foel Goch, a summit arbitrarily ignored in favour of a well-worn path to its side because it fails to reach the magic 3000ft. It is a simple summit in itself, and yet has a northern cwm that is rich with neglected complications.

Y Garn is soon underfoot. It seems the day moves beneath your feet while your head is engaged elsewhere. This then is the familiar Glyders: people on summits, whose faces you will not recall; lake shapes in cwms, with names you know; and black north crags, with climbers somewhere on them, calling to each other. The high sun casts you and your shadow as a small and insignificant patch on the ground; recollections of other times here crowd in on you and further diminish the significance of being here today.

The descent to Llyn y Cŵn is a romp: a great, galloping rush down a slope unhindered by anything except a ridiculous wire fence and its stile. The lake itself could be thought of as a halfway house of this particular

Looking back towards Y Garn, Foel Goch and Mynydd Perfedd from Glyder Fach

Above: *A rocky descent from Glyder Fach precedes a gentle traverse of the ridge's grassy eastern arm (Route B2)*

Below: *Looking back towards Glyder Fach from Llyn y Caseg Fraith on Route B2*

Above: *The grassy eastern arm of Route B2 seen from above Capel Curig*

Below: *Summit of Glyder Fawr; looking towards Glyder Fach*

walk. And of others, too, judging by the numbers of people who stop here to drink, or simply to sit with elbows on knees, staring at dusty boots. But be warned: this being the lowest col on the ridge, and with the long ascent to Glyder Fawr ahead, the threat to morale is enormous.

This, the north-west slope of Glyder Fawr, is the cruellest in all the Glyders. Ordinary people are seen to assume the hunted crouch of shot hyena (not the laughing kind) as they jerk and slither through the long, hot afternoon. Those whose movements and temperament happen to result in net upward progress are later found grinning ridiculously from high perches among the many piles of stones which litter the summit area, and showing few signs of ever wanting to come down again. *But is it worth the effort? Don't* ever *ask.*

By now the sun has come full round; while the ridge itself has passed the angle of the dogleg and heads due east, dropping all the way. The day, so soon begun, is nearly lost and gone.

All who pass over the Glyder plateau act out private little fantasies there. So that even on empty winter days, when hoar frost masks out the familiar landmarks, it is not so much of a wilderness as a wilderness waiting: a bus station at dawn; a market place on Sunday; an empty stage; and nothing you do will make it any different. The fantastic wilderness is nowhere but in your head.

A sense of urgency overwhelms the moment. Castell y Gwynt passes by in a rush, the imminent sunset over Snowdon an unsung masterpiece at your back. Even the summit of Glyder Fach is, without regret or redress, left untouched. No time for it; not today. No need either; not when you have done what you have done, and seen what you have seen.

Tripping through the bear traps, tired of caution, you will go down to the shore of a limitless ocean of grass. I challenge anyone who doubts the inherent sensuality of grass to come here, at this time of day, at the end of this walk, and plunge both feet into that sea while denying that truth. Unfortunately, as with all self-indulgent

behaviour, the novelty must pale sooner or later. With this one it is sooner – at the bogs of Llyn y Caseg Fraith. What might have been a romantic stroll through the sunset of your day is reduced to something rather less when there's a pound of slutch clinging to each foot.

And still there's miles to go; out along and down along – a lingering arm that will not release its grip until it has wrung every last drop of determination from your miserable little body. The world, meanwhile, has turned: headlights flicker along the Dyffryn Mymbyr; black pools fill the Ogwen Valley; and the lights of Capel Curig glitter untouchably like those of a Christmas tree in a shop window. Never mind: if you are very, very lucky you may yet find a safe way through the crags at the end of the ridge. And wouldn't *that* be nice.

Foel Goch (right) from Pen yr Ole Wen; Y Garn on left, Elidir Fawr in the right background

C: THE SNOWDON GROUP

Enough has been said already on the abuse of Snowdon not to have to repeat it at length here. And yet so grand is the setting that no amount of trash or traffic on the summit cone will detract completely from the simple delight of standing on the highest peak in Wales.

Not that Snowdon or any of its satellites could ever be thought of as *elegant* mountains, abused or not. Quite simply this is because the group – notwithstanding a number of classical profiles from a distance – is typified by the original lumpish peak, a slope of red scree funnelling into a lake as unfriendly as a sterile glacier pool.

Rock climbing is not associated with Snowdon itself, although surrounding peaks can boast some of the best crags in Britain. Of these, Clogwyn du'r Arddu maintains a reputation as one of the very best mountain crags; while

The Snowdon Horseshoe (Route C1) viewed from Capel Curig. In these conditions the route demands winter climbing equipment and skills

even the hugely unpopular north-east face of Lliwedd retains a faithful band of adherents. Less obviously good are the crags of Cwm Glas – Dinas Mot, Cyrn Las, Clogwyn y Ddysgl – which prove to have climbs of equally enduring quality.

Extra altitude accounts for Snowdon's winter popularity. A strip of snow clings tenaciously to the bed of Parsley Fern Gully – the classic winter exit from Upper Cwm Glas – long after many of the classic Glyder and Carneddau gullies have wilted away. The Central Trinity couloir of Snowdon's north face is equally persistent. Unfortunately, extra problems arising from these conditions are frequently underestimated. Even normal walking tracks like the Pig and Watkin can become inordinately dangerous under snow; whereas the ridges themselves suffer proportionately greater change of character. Crib Goch, for instance, under *any* kind of winter conditions – verglas, powder, nevé – will be a daunting experience to anyone unfamiliar with the equipment or techniques essential for the traverse. Every winter it dispatches a life or two down its flanks.

Extracting the best from Snowdon also calls for a shrewd sense of timing. The Horseshoe and other normal ascent routes are always busy between 9 a.m. and 5 p.m. in summer, and on off-season weekends; whereas fringe areas – Yr Aran and Moel Eilio – are usually quiet at any time.

C1: THE SNOWDON HORSESHOE

Justifiably one of the most famous ridge scrambles in Britain.

Distance/Time:
12km (7½ miles). 6 hours.

Ascent:
1050m (3500ft)

Major Summits:
Grib Goch – 921m (3022ft)
Crib y Ddysgl/Garnedd Ugain – 1065m (3495ft)
Snowdon/Yr Wyddfa – 1085m (3559ft)
Lliwedd – 898m (2947ft)

The Snowdon Horseshoe (Route C1) in summer conditions.
The normal ascent of Crib Goch (right) begins up the blunt
East Ridge (facing), while variant C1(a) takes the North Ridge
on the right skyline. The descent from Lliwedd (left) follows
the partially sunlit ridge leading from left to centre left,
while variant C1(b) descends Y Gribin, the sunlit ridge
in the centre

Terrain:
Bare rock ridges connected by good paths.

Main Summer Difficulties:
Exposed scrambling up to and along Crib Goch.

Winter Conditions:
A winter climb, not a scramble. In good, deep snow conditions it gives a magnificent if serious outing.

Emergency Alternatives:
Descent north into Cwm Glas Bach from Bwlch Coch (621552). See also Variants (b) and (c).

Special Problems:
Strong winds on Crib Goch. This is a common and serious problem, and the route is best avoided in those conditions.

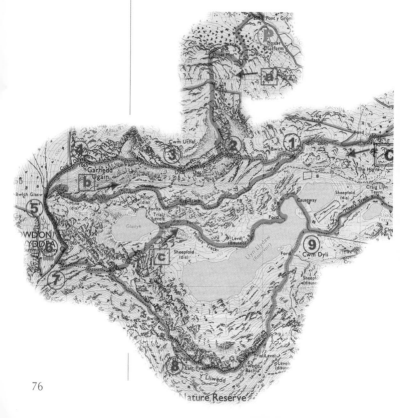

Approach:
Along the A4086 between Llanberis and its junction with
the A498 Beddgelert to Capel Curig road.

Start:
Pen y Pass (647556). Car park (fee) usually full after
9.30a.m. at weekends.

Finish:
As above.

ROUTE DESCRIPTION

From the upper car park, follow the Pig Track westwards
– rising steadily – to Bwlch y Moch[1] (633553). Turn right
(west) and follow a good path over a shoulder to the start
of the steep east ridge to Crib Goch summit. (Technically,
the highest part of the ridge is some way towards Crib y
Ddysgl, but this eastern extremity is a better landmark.)
The ascent is fairly straightforward by its easiest route,
though this is not always easy to find. The best choice
lies almost directly up the crest; and the rock
here is also the soundest. The ridge
emerges almost exactly at the 'summit'[2]
(1¾ hrs).

The Crib Goch itself heads off westwards and is almost horizontal. Narrow
and intimidating at first acquaintance,
the key is to stay as high as possible,
using the actual crest for handholds. As
the Pinnacles approach, a variant goes
down left but finds more trouble than it
avoids. Instead, keep close to the crest and
dodge through them with some exposed but
straightforward scrambling. A small scree gully finally
leads down onto the deliciously flat Bwlch Coch[3] (½ hr).

The ridge narrows again as it ascends Crib y Ddysgl.
Various obstacles present themselves, though again it is
best to stay near the crest. The ridge gradually broadens
to the summit area and trig point[4] (¾ hr).

A gentle circuit around the lip of the cwm, passing
the Pig Track marker post (608549),[5] leads onto the
railway and so to Snowdon Summit[6] (¼ hr).

Follow the South Ridge (actually south-west) down

77

from the summit for about 200m to a marker post. Turn down left here and follow the track – the Watkin – to level ground at Bwlch y Saethau.[7] Continue directly to ascend Lliwedd by its north-west ridge[8] (1¼ hrs).

Continue along a good path above the cliff top, following it down a steep and tricky slope to level ground at Llyn Llydaw and a junction with the Miners' Track[9] (634546). Follow this back to Pen y Pass (1½ hrs).

It is June – the hesitant month – and the day still shivers from its cold clasp dawn; a clear good day in parenthesis, a jewel in the mud of a year. At Pen y Pass the first arrivals have begun stamping familiarity into their stiff boots; assessing, meanwhile, the weather prospects with sharp intakes of air. Nothing is certain. Hailstones, even, forged on tall anvil clouds of the afternoon, might yet flurry from the sky, bouncing softly in spring grass, harshly on the rock. There is a sudden mounting excitement in their voices as they turn to begin their ascent of the Pig Track, loose stones spitting from their heels as rucsac straps are settled on the move. Their day, only just begun, is already out of breath.

Bwlch y Moch is the first test of will-power. It would be so easy to dally at this picturesque saddle with its

The blunt East Ridge of Crib Goch seen from Bwlch y Moch (Route C1)

surprise view of Lliwedd and Llyn Llydaw. From here the Pig Track continues gently across the hillside towards the inner cirque below Snowdon; whereas the path to begin the Horseshoe rises abruptly rightwards to zig-zag improbably up the grim red rocks of Crib Goch's east ridge. Caution argues for the Pig Track; ambition for the Horseshoe.

An exposed traverse on the East Ridge of Crib Goch (Route C1)

79

A traffic jam has built up at the first steepening. Three anxious faces peer down from a ledge some fifteen feet above the base. A fourth, creased with uncertainty, mouths plaintive replies towards them. This last face belongs to a middle-aged man who, by the sole support of lilywhite fingers curled over an edge, holds his blubbery body in a state of unstable equilibrium. This is a sorry business all round. People waiting below are unsure of what to do. Mostly they look away politely, or pretend to rummage in their rucsacs. Time goes on. A clutter of boys and girls arrive and scramble past impatiently. In a loud voice, one of the boys asks his teacher if the man is going to fall off. Can this really be happening on these easy rocks on this sunny day? The leader of the group recently arrived puts down his rucsac, goes straight to the man's side, taps a hold with his finger, and says: 'Put your foot here.' And to everyone's surprise, that is exactly what the man does. In seconds he has rejoined his companions on the higher ledge. 'You went the wrong way that's all,' says the leader, pre-empting an unnecessary apology. For a few moments the saved man is torn between self-recrimination and nervous levity. In the end he smiles

Approaching the Pinnacles on the traverse of Crib Goch (Route C1). The route continues over Crib y Ddysgl (right) then ascends easily to the summit of Snowdon

and makes a joke – it doesn't matter what it was. Probably he will now enjoy his day. So will we.

An unearthly atmosphere envelops Crib Goch Summit. Lost souls gather here to await decisions on their destiny – little parcels of humanity dumped at the sorting office of the afterlife. Here begins a perilous journey: a conveyor belt crossing of Crib Goch towards Crib y Ddysgl and salvation. One by one the people board and are carried off into the distance, their places in the queue filled by those more recently elevated. Drawn helplessly into the hiatus at the Pinnacles, the bobbing people-parcels cling desperately to the belt now contorted into a roller-coaster ride of violent ups and down. Some survive, some don't; but head counts must wait until Bwlch Coch, the grassy haven beyond, where at last is space enough to lie down without being accused by your companions of showing off.

The thing is only half done. Whereas the Crib y Ddysgl section ahead is no less of a ridge, it is – for some reason – much less memorable; which may go some way towards explaining why even veterans manage to get themselves lost. Bravely we tackle everything the ridge

Looking back towards the Pinacles of Crib Goch (Route C1)

The ascent of Crib y Ddysgl (Route C1). Crib Goch in the background

can throw at us; while others, full of cunning, skirt these obstacles along flanking paths and are never seen again.

Winter changes the middle Ddysgl ridge into a grim mountainside. Snow-covered rocks on the Cwm Glas side are too easy and extensive to warrant total caution; and yet far too insecure to suffer a casual approach. Now, in summer, the ridge is quite straightforward – even a fraction tedious – although it does try to improve itself towards the end. As with Crib Goch, the summit itself is unremarkable; as a result most people prefer to call the peak by the name of its ridge than by Garnedd Ugain, the name of its highest point. Further evidence that mountaineers care less for destinations than journeys undertaken to reach them.

It's a doddle down to the Pig Track. Here, against the standing stone which marks its exit, one may lounge in studied arrogance while the sweaty bodies of mere walkers emerge from the deep. *'Nice day for it'* is the greeting which appears to elicit the most withered facial expressions. At your back, meanwhile, not a dozen strides away, a column of pilgrims on the Llanberis Path moves on: too many to greet, too many to count. And so, whichever way we came to be here, we now all have a common path and a common purpose. Rucsacs and

handbags, boots and sandals, ropes and frisbees, all mixed up together. Snowdon Summit here we come.

And what do we find? We find something more like a seagull nesting colony than a mountain top. Every available perch is taken up by a masticating mountaineer. From time to time, one of them will jerk itself upright, flutter its arms, belch, and take off for the blue distance; only to be replaced by another, indistinguishable in behaviour from the one just departed. Unlike seagulls, however, appearances among Snowdon Summiteers can vary greatly. Where else can you see duvet waistcoats side by side with bikinis, and each worn with equal panache and propriety?

The micro environment of the summit café is no less bizarre. That people who have expended so much in getting to the top – whether it be effort on the walk or money on the train – should choose to celebrate by dining in this place is an irony of unlimited interest to amateur philosophers. The only rational explanation is that these people are penitents enjoying the climax of their flagellation. I hope it hurts.

Now for a little trick. Unless you want to fritter away the rest of a perfectly good afternoon doing good deeds for people, do *not* descend directly to Bwlch y Saethau

View from Snowdon summit towards Lliwedd, the final objective of Route 'C1

along with misdirected and ill-shod tourists heading for Beddgelert. Why? Because that slope is set exactly at the critical angle for human beings in unsuitable footwear. Normally, of course, most of these people will proceed

Lliwedd

downwards according to the law of acceleration down an inclined plane; but there's always a few who will discover that as long as they keep very still, they are able to hold position on the slope indefinitely – or at least until rescued (by you, if you go that way). The trick, then, is to descend the South Ridge as far as the Watkin marker stone, and to follow that path down to the Bwlch instead – falling bodies permitted. Simple.

Because the Horseshoe is so varied and interesting, it is easy to ignore the cumulative effect of all that scrambling. Now, faced with an untimely ascent of Lliwedd, you suddenly feel well and truly knackered. Enough is enough. But enough isn't always enough in the mountains: even when overtaken by weariness, the nightmare plod up Lliwedd is considered a mandatory experience. It is time for another trick. By tracking leftwards to follow the very edge of the ridge, and by breathing on cold upwellings from the shadowed north face, it is just possible – even at this late stage – to frighten yourself into vitality. Scrambling addicts know all about this ploy. Anyway, by placing your psyche on the knife edge of intoxication, you are able to cheat fatigue by entering a state of heightened awareness. It gets you to the top in no time at all.

Alone on Lliwedd. Where have all the others gone? The actual summit will remain inviolate today; not in respect of the gods who dwell here – for heaven knows they don't deserve it – but because it is infested by a swarm of exotic bugs encouraged upwards by a promise of moisture. Round and round they go, dizzied by the dance until they flop in their thousands onto the stones of the path where their fat bellies are squashed underfoot like fallen blackcurrants.

The slow spiral down to Llyn Llydaw and the Miners' is accompanied by that memory, that...sensation. Disgust and elation all rolled into one: an appropriate *thought for the day*.

A less popular, though equally difficult, start to the Horseshoe.

VARIANT (A):
CRIB GOCH NORTH RIDGE

Distance/Time:
Little difference from the normal way.

Terrain:
Steep scree to a narrow rock ridge.

Main Summer Difficulties:
Scrambling on the upper section of the ridge.

Winter Conditions:
Similar to the normal route. Not recommended.

Special Problems:
Route-finding to gain the start of the ridge.

Start:
Pont y Gromlech (629566). Parking for early starters.

Finish:
Crib Goch Summit (626553).

ROUTE DESCRIPTION

Go over the stile near the bridge and follow a path up to a smooth cone of rock – *The Nose* of Dinas Mot. Now go steeply up left, keeping just below the cliffs, on a difficult path over scree and boulders. The angle eventually eases at a small grass- and boulder-filled depression. Trend right at the top of this to find a path which contours rightwards across the hillside to heather slopes above the cliffs of Dinas Mot.

The ridge is broad at first, offering many choices of line. Higher, it narrows to a rock knife edge. There is some loose rock here, so it is best to stay as near to the crest as possible. However, the difficulty soon eases and a junction is reached with the normal route at Crib Goch Summit.

VARIANT (B):
PIG TRACK DESCENT

A cop out! In practice, an interesting way down and not that much shorter than the full horseshoe.

Distance/Time:
Reduces overall distance by 1½ km (1 mile) and saves 1 hour.

Terrain:
Well-maintained path with some rocky sections.

Main Summer Difficulties:
None.

Winter Conditions:
Upper section – the Zig-Zags – subject to severe drifting.
Exit sometimes corniced.

Start:
Snowdon Summit.

Finish:
Pen y Pass.

ROUTE DESCRIPTION

Return from summit to Pig Track marker post (607548).
Follow the recently improved Zig-Zags down towards
Glaslyn; but instead of continuing down to the lake (as
for the Miners' Track), contour the hillside eastwards. The
path is mostly good, though interspersed with occasional
rock bluffs of no difficulty. The line is maintained to
Bwlch y Moch, beyond which it descends steadily to Pen
y Pass.

VARIANT (C):
Y GRIBIN DESCENT

Distance/Time:
Not much shorter but saves about ½ hour.

Terrain:
A bare rock ridge followed by a broad track.

Main Summer Difficulties:
Scrambling down Y Gribin itself.

Winter Conditions:
Does not hold snow well. Not recommended.

Special Problems:
Locating top of ridge.

Start:
Bwlch y Saethau (615542).

Finish:
Pen y Pass.

An interesting ridge
scramble which, in
combination with
Crib Goch, provides
an alternative
Horseshoe of no less
quality.

Looking back up Y Gribin, variant descent C1(c)

ROUTE DESCRIPTION

From the level section of Bwlch y Saethau, probe cautiously north-east to locate the protruding rock shoulder which betrays the start of the ridge. The general line of descent on the ridge is obvious; although there can be problems with the intricacies of route-finding. The best route stays near the crest, making only occasional diversions for the obvious difficulties. The ridge finally levels out at the east shore of Glaslyn. The Miners' Track is on the far side of the outflow and is followed down to Pen y Pass.

C2: SNOWDON: THE MAIN TRAVERSE

A long traverse crossing the Snowdon group from Beddgelert to Llanberis.

Distance/Time:
20km (12½ miles). 7 hours.

Ascent:
1850m (6100ft)

Major Summits:
Yr Aran – 747m (2451ft)
Snowdon/Yr Wyddfa – 1085m (3559ft)
Moel Cynghorion – 672m (2207ft)
Foel Goch – 605m (1983ft)
Foel Gron – 629m (2063ft)
Moel Eilio – 726m (2382ft)

Terrain:
Grass tracks/paths or rocky paths.

Main Summer Difficulties:
Short, easy scrambling sections on upper South Ridge.

Winter Conditions:
Exhausting and impractical in anything other than light cover or well-consolidated conditions. Bwlch Main can become a narrow snow arête.

Emergency Alternatives:
Descent north or south from Bwlch Maesgwm (572559); see also Variants (a), (b) and (c).

Special Problems:
Route-finding north of Snowdon in bad visibility. Transport can also be a problem – buses run only in summer and are infrequent.

(continued on following page)

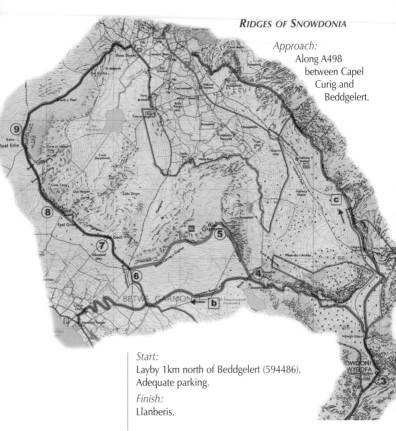

Approach:
Along A498 between Capel Curig and Beddgelert.

Start:
Layby 1km north of Beddgelert (594486). Adequate parking.

Finish:
Llanberis.

ROUTE DESCRIPTION

From the layby, a narrow path goes through a gate near garages and zig-zags up to a level section and wall. At a sharp bend in the wall, go right, through a gate, and cross a field to another gate. A track leads left to a farm, but instead go uphill, through another gate, and continue near a stream to reach the skyline. Go through a final gate on the left and so gain a broad ridge leading up to a subsidiary summit and cairn (other approach paths arrive here). Continue along the narrowing ridge to the summit of Yr Aran[1] (1¾ hrs).

Continue down the far ridge until, just before a stile

is reached, the path cuts back down left and descends to
the col at the start of Snowdon South Ridge[2] (605522).
Follow the well-worn path due north, rising steadily along
the crest of the South Ridge. The ridge narrows at a
subsidiary summit, and again shortly after at Bwlch Main
where the Beddgelert Path arrives. Follow the ridge,
swinging slightly east, over rocks to Snowdon Summit[3]
(1¾ hrs).

First follow the railway line northwards; but then bear
left at a marker stone as for the Snowdon Ranger and zig-
zag down to Bwlch Cwm Brwynog[4] (591557). A steep
grass ridge goes directly from here up to the broad
summit area of Moel Cynghorion[5] (1hr).

Follow the shallow ridge west, dipping to Bwlch
Maesgwm.[6] A stile begins an ascent of Foel Goch; the
best route following a line left then right to the summit.[7]
From the col beyond, the ridge to Foel Gron[8] is better
defined. A narrow grass neck beyond that summit leads
onto a more open ridge up to Moel Eilio summit[9]
(1½ hrs).

Take the path north down a blunt ridge to Bwlch y

*On Yr Aran, the first
objective on Route C2*

91

Groes (557599) or go north-west down a ridge to Hafod Uchaf (573591). Either way leads into Llanberis (1 hr).

Some people will tell you that Beddgelert is no longer a proper village; that the grime of real life has been scrubbed off its streets. That may well be so. It may also be true that old women with bent backs are getting a little thin on the ground here of late. Not many asthmatic miners either… No-one denies the place has been eaten up by tourism; but these hotels, holiday homes, gift shops, and even the fake Gelert legend have been part of the place for such a long time that the coming and going of a Beddgelert tourist season seems no less a natural phenomenon than the ebb and flow of a Grimsby tide. Facades of quaintness are erected here as anywhere else, and will tell you little of the realities they hide. Besides, tourists make much more interesting subjects for superficial observation that gritty natives, particularly when our present interest in Beddgelert extends no deeper than as a place to park a car.

The beginnings of this particular route up Yr Aran are pastoral and diversionary in the extreme: Snowdon seems

The Nantlle Ridge and Mynydd Mawr seen from the col between Yr Aran and the start of Snowdon's South Ridge on Route C2

a very long way indeed (it would: it is). *And there isn't even a need to climb Yr Aran!* Ahah, but this is *good* for you. As with school Latin, it is inconsequential labour of this sort that has made Britain what it is today. It intensifies the warm glow of worthiness.

Picture a lone figure – it could be a man – moving slowly up a hillside. You are watching him from above; from a balloon perhaps. The sun is in the south-east – an autumn sun barely risen above the wedged profiles of distant mountains. It backlights the mist settled in hollows during the night, and makes patches on frosty meadows. The man, intent on his climb, sees none of this. He walks with effort, as if wading a shallow sea, towards the cairn of his mountain. He sees only the waves of grass parting beneath his feet. Behind him, the sunlight rakes across the face of a nearby mountain, remodelling its ungainly features into a fine and unusual profile. In a moment or two the sculpture will melt, lost again to the shadow and haze for another day, perhaps another year. The man seems completely unconcerned by what is going on around him. You cup your hands to call down to him. He stops and looks up at you with his quizzical, pantomime face.

The second leg of Route C2 seen from Snowdon's South Ridge. The route ascends both Moel Cynghorion (centre right) and Moel Eilio (centre left)

The view east from Snowdon summit on Route C2. Crib Goch is on the left; Llyn Llydaw below; Moel Siabod in the background

'Behind you!' you shout, pointing excitedly towards the south. He shakes his head and grins his exaggerated grin: 'You can't fool me!' he says, proceeding with his climb.

Yr Aran is a private affair. Something you do just for yourself before doing what you have to do; which is to go up to Snowdon like everyone else. Snowdon is in view now, its summit hotel glinting in the sun like a beer can on a football stadium terrace, its South Ridge supporters thickening by the minute. Hear the chant? *Snow-don! Snow-don!* But between you and it is a deep col. So, you have not begun at all. To begin you must first go down the shadow of Yr Aran. Down where the rocks are still icy from the night. Down to where people sit and look up, the sun in their eyes, wondering what starts the stones rolling, each time you slip. Yes: right down there. Is Yr Aran no longer a private affair?

Snowdon South Ridge is not a chore. Momentum accumulated on Yr Aran will at least get you over the first knoll, and after that it's a gift – honest. Mostly the ridge is broad and uneventful, until a short diversion brings you to the edge of a great cliff. Peering over the lip you see a jumble of tottering, deserted crags. No climbers: no calls. Only the wind sifting through clumps of coarse grass that

cling in improbable places. An indeterminate distance below is the reluctantly grazed basin of Cwm Tregalan; and beyond that only the scattered toytown rectangles of ruined quarry buildings, the thin ribbon of the Watkin Path winding between them like a sandpit roadway. You could lose a whole boxful of Dinkies down there.

Bwlch Main signals the change to a more rugged experience. At a subsidiary peak the path narrows, turns to rock, and holds its breath across the slender ridge. This is where the Beddgelert Path arrives, and between them they find a winding trail through the split blocks towards the final cone. The café is locked up and deserted; the railway lines that feed it quietly rusting beneath an early drift. Off-season days at Snowdon Summit are so very different from the usual crush. There may a hundred or more people here at times like this, and it can be as quiet as a church. Following the railway northward (for once with impunity), the rest of the traverse can be seen laid out before you: first the barren scree back of the immediate ridge; then a procession of gentle hills; and finally the misty green shape of Moel Eilio.

This is the Snowdon Ranger, hurrying down to Llyn Cwellyn with scant regard for ridges – or indeed anything

The cliffs of Clogwyn Du'r Arddu seen from Route C2

95

Looking back towards Snowdon summit from Moel Cynghorion on Route C2

else of interest. It has its uses, though, so follow it to where it swings west before breaking off at a tangent, arriving at the true ridge where it overlooks Cwm Brwynog. The tiny pool of Llyn du'r Arddu is far below, reflecting a raindrop of blue in the shadow of Clogwyn du'r Arddu, the most enigmatic of Snowdonia's big cliffs. There is only a tantalising glimpse of its wall from here – a vertical pillar known as the East Gully Wall – but its great presence is felt nevertheless.

The Ranger is abandoned for good at Bwlch Cwm Brwynog. The path from here onwards – when there is a path – will be along a train of small hills. Moel Cynghorion, the first of them, has a fine sounding name worth learning to pronounced but an unpronounceable ridge to its summit. Puffing up two hundred metres of featureless grass proves to be only fractionally more interesting than watching it grow; and grass grows very slowly at this altitude. But surely this is a small price to pay for your very own mountain range.

At a high pass beyond Cynghorion is a ghostly thoroughfare: tracks without vehicles, telegraph poles without wires, paths without people. There is a quick way down to Llanberis from here, or south to rejoin the Ranger path; but a strange spell is being worked, so that you will find yourself toiling uphill again – to Foel Goch; and again – to Foel Gron; and again – to Moel Eilio. The process is addictive. On Eilio, when suddenly you realise there are no more hills to climb, the sense of elation is subdued by an even greater sense of loss. Of course, you could always turn and walk back to Beddgelert...

And so finally to Llanberis, a village that should satisfy even the most critical seekers of authenticity. Unlike Beddgelert, there is nothing quaint about *this* place. Quite the contrary, in fact, because here tourists are shunted off the to village perimeter as soon as possible: to the dirty old quarries; to the smelly railway yards; and to all manner of other 'attractions' that only Wales and the Welsh could promote, and only England and the English could enjoy. The fact that every jack one of them is shut for winter hardly seems to matter.

Ruined farm in Cwm Brwynog below Moel Cynghorion (route C2)

97

A pleasant alternative
start if Yr Aran is to
be avoided.

VARIANT (A): DIRECT APPROACH TO SOUTH RIDGE

Distance/Miles:
Reduces distance only by 1½ km (1 mile), but saves more
than 1 hour.

Terrain:
Track and good paths.

Main Summer Difficulties:
None.

Winter Conditions:
Not usually affected.

Start:
Pont Bethania car park on A498 (627506).

Finish:
Bwlch Cwm Llan (605522).

ROUTE DESCRIPTION

Cross the main road and follow the lane north to where
a well-marked stone track bears left through trees. After
winding up the hillside near the stream, it passes through
the narrows of the cwm as a raised trackway. Just beyond
the narrows, where the path levels out before it crosses
the stream, bear left to reach a level track – an old
tramway – on the left-bounding hillside. Follow this for a
few hundred metres; then bear left again, rising steadily
across the slope, to reach the South Ridge just above
Bwlch Cwm Llan.

Completes a shorter
traverse of Snowdon,
avoiding the Eilio
group.

VARIANT (B): DESCENT OF SNOWDON RANGER

Distance/Time:
Reduces overall distance by 6km (4 miles) and saves 2
hours.

Terrain:
A broad, well-maintained path.

Main Summer Difficulties:
None.

Winter Conditions:
No added problems in relation to original route.

Start:
Bwlch Cwm Brwynog (591557).

Finish:
Snowdon Ranger car park (565551).

ROUTE DESCRIPTION

Instead of breaking off to reach Bwlch Cwm Brwynog, continue along the main path, dropping gently, to the slopes above Llyn Cwellyn. (The path down from Bwlch Maesgwm arrives here.) A zig-zag descent leads to farm buildings; and a track from those, after a slight diversion, leads to the main road and car park.

VARIANT (C): DIRECT DESCENT TO LLANBERIS

A pleasant and surprisingly neglected ridge walk.

Distance/Time:
Reduces overall distance by 4km (2½ miles), saving 1½ hours.

Terrain:
Stone track, then a pathless grass ridge.

Main Summer Difficulties:
None

Winter Conditions:
No added problems.

Special Problems:
Detailed route-finding in bad visibility – no cairns or path.

Start:
Snowdon Summit.

Finish:
Llanberis.

ROUTE DESCRIPTION

Instead of veering off the railway, as for the Snowdon Ranger, continue along it and the main path which follows – the Llanberis Path – to where it passes beneath the railway near Clogwyn Station (608561). Leave the path and follow the railway for a few hundred metres until beyond the subsidiary summit of Llechog (a fine viewpoint and worth the short diversion). Leave the

The variant descent C2(c) from Snowdon (centre left) follows the grassy ridge leading down to the town of Llanberis by the lake

railway and follow the main ridge crest along comfortable grass and with fine views down into Llanberis Pass. Beyond another subsidiary top, the ridge becomes less well defined and drops to a broad, marshy col. The Llanberis Path can be seen down left from here, but it is worth continuing over the final hump before trending down left to join it a short distance before its end. Follow the surfaced road down to the main road into Llanberis.

D: THE MOELWYNS

The Moelwyns have never attained notoriety. A picture
has emerged over the years of an area unworthy of serious
attention, and this is despite a collection of rewarding
walks and climbs to advertise its many qualities. Perhaps
it is the thrust of industry into a mountain landscape that
leaves so unsavoury a taste in the aesthete's mouth. And
what else when a dam wall can be seen cutting across
the floor of a remote cwm; when slate tips replace screes
below a fine crag; or when a high col is disfigured by an
abandoned terrace of quarrymen's lodgings? Enjoyment
of the Moelwyns depends very much on your reaction to
these and other artefacts. Many people are disgusted;
others turn a blind eye; while some welcome them as a
uniquely interesting feature of the region.

Because the high ground is much less rugged than
on Snowdon or the Glyders, most of the good rock
climbing is confined to isolated crags on the lower south
and west slopes. By far the best of them are those which
line the hillside above Blaenau Ffestiniog. Solid rock,
a moderate angle, and a profusion of holds combine
to make these crags ideal for climbers of modest ability
or ambition. They are much more appropriate, for
instance, than the polished and oversubscribed climbs at
Idwal.

By contrast, winter climbing is poorly represented.
There are a few short gullies set at respectable altitude
above Llyn y Foel on Moel Siabod; but even they are
unable to survive their south-easterly aspect for very long.
Winter walking is also less good than might be supposed.
Ironically, the problem lies not so much with the difficulty
of terrain as with its gentleness. A shortage of exposed
ridges means that snowfall, instead of being blown clear
of the high ground, as often happens in the Carneddau,
tends to lie more or less where it falls, making the walks
very laborious indeed. Add to this the problems of
crossing untracked marshy ground that is covered in
snow, along with the very real possibility of disappearing

down a hidden mine shaft, and the attraction soon begins to pall.

The Moelwyns are at their best during crisp, calm days in spring or autumn, when the ground is dry or frozen, and the sensation of great space is not dulled by low cloud. At such times there is no question of inferiority.

D1: MOELWYNS: NORTHERN RIDGES

Distance/Time:
28km (17½ miles). 8 hours.

Ascent:
1300m (4300ft)

Major Summits:
Moel Siabod – 872m (2861ft)
Moel Meirch – 607m (1990ft)
Moel Druman – 676m (2217ft)
Allt Fawr – 697m (2287ft)

Terrain:
Forest tracks, rock ridge, grass paths, and a surfaced road to finish. Bogs.

Main Summer Difficulties:
Short sections of scrambling on Daear Ddu. Length.

Winter Conditions:
Best under light snow cover. Well-consolidated deep snow conditions are rare.

Emergency Alternatives:
Descent to A498 from Bwlch y Rhediad (665524).

A long traverse down
the spine of the
Moelwyns and based
on Dolwyddelan.

Special Problems:
Ground becomes very boggy during periods of poor weather. Route-finding in bad visibility can be extremely difficult.

Approach:
Along A470 between Betws y Coed and Bleanau Ffestiniog.

Start:
Dolwyddelan crossroads (735524). Adequate parking.

Finish:
As above (or at head of Crimea Pass (700487) on A470).

ROUTE DESCRIPTION

Follow the narrow uphill road from the cross-roads to a T-junction. Turn right and then, after less than 100m, go left through a gate to cross a field and reach another gate. Through this, then follow a track on the left – over a bog – to a fine viewpoint on a grass knoll. The track continues by a stile and stepping-stones until it swings right, crosses another stile, and enters forestry land. Follow the path through trees, over a footbridge, to reach the main forest track. Follow this for about 1km until beyond where it crosses a stream by a concrete bridge. The main track curves right, but turn left here and follow this track, trending right, to a terminus.[1] Ford the stream and follow the rocky path through trees to a stile leading out onto open ground. Follow the narrow, winding path to Llyn y Foel[2] (1½ hrs).

Over on the left is the obvious east ridge (Daear Ddu) leading directly, with occasional sections of scrambling, to the summit of Moel Siabod[3] (¾ hr).

Go down the long, grass ridge westwards to a boggy col and stile.[4] A gradual rise up to Carnedd y Cribiau[5] is best taken on the left where there is a reasonable path. Continue, descending gradually, to the boggy col of Bwlch y Rhediad.[6] A gradual rise now to Moel Meirch[7] and, on its left side, Llyn Edno[8] (2¼ hrs).

Trend left to gain the Ysgafell Wen (which is really the continuation of Yr Arddu, a parallel ridge on the left). Follow the crest until a narrow path curves up left to Moel

103

Moel Siabod and the northern Moelwyn ridge seen from Crib Goch

Druman.[9] Descend and pass Llyn Conglog on its left before rising to the narrow summit ridge of Allt Fawr[10] overlooking slate quarries (1½ hrs).

Go down steeply north-east, following a grass ridge, to gain a track leading to the crest of the Crimea Pass.[11] Turn left to reach Dolwyddelan in 6km. (2 hours).

I was determined to be alone for this one, and had gone to *extraordinary lengths* to be alone. Even the dog had been left behind, sulking. It was a midweek day in April, the ground frozen hard from a cloudless night.

Dolwyddelan was under a mist. As if on cue, the people of the village began emptying one by one from the doors of their stone houses to begin, each in their different ways, their different day. A chained farm dog barked out its hollow, spasmodic cough. I doubt if a film director could have orchestrated a more poignant dawn.

Not far above the misty influence of the village, at a tiny hill, came an unexpected preview of the route ahead. Dominating the near horizon, beyond a great tract of rough grazing land, stood the huge wedge of Moel Siabod – first and highest objective of the day. Then, tracking south, the line of the whole ridge could be discerned, rising above the high moorland base that supported it. A tiny white peak above its skyline proved to be the distant snow-capped summit of Snowdon: the scale of the enterprise, which up until now had been grossly underestimated, suddenly slotted into place.

The path veered unexpectedly towards the forest and delved inside, dodging between trees and darting over narrow footbridges. Hastening to follow, I wondered if I – like Hansel – ought to be laying a trail of stones to facilitate my escape (but if he was such a ripe banana, what possessed him to lead Gretel back to the wicked stepmother?). It must have been while trying to solve this

Llyn y Foel and the Daear Ddu ridge to Moel Siabod (Route D1)

The view west from the summit of Moel Siabod. The broad ridge continuation ridge of Route D1 can be seen veering south

paradox that I became lost. Now being lost in Forestry Commission forest is no ordinarily exasperating business: there are many roads; these many roads all look the same; and what is more, these many same-looking roads all lead back onto the road you were on twenty minutes previously. I have proof. Sometimes, and as if they hadn't already got enough trees, the Commission will plant clean across one of its own roads. This extinguishes any lingering faith you may have in your map reading ability. Trying to follow these roads falls lower down the thera- peutic scale than forcing a golf ball up your nostril; and trying to make sense out of the Commission's special *circular* roads – a forestry equivalent of a Black Hole – is on a par with using a five iron to get it out again. I can only guess that the foresters eventually get bored fooling around; which was how I came to be dumped at the far side with an uninterrupted view across the hinterland towards Moel Siabod; and which – for all the time I had spent getting there – looked not a whole lot closer.

Llyn y Foel was breathtaking. Calmed by a pane of ice in each bay, the waters reflected the perfect propor- tions of the Daear Ddu ridge and its sweep to the summit.

What a ridge: easy scrambling, sound rock, elegant line. Add sun and solitude and you have an unbeatable formula.

The marshy ridge between Moel Siabod and Moel Meirch (Route B1)

This precious ridge would have to be recorded. Now since human participation would be a necessary part of the photographic record, and since – you remember – I had contrived to be alone, it meant that it would have to be one of those delayed release photos. Okay, the first job was to find a suitable boulder on which to rest the camera. That would be easy – the ridge was full of them. However, for reasons now unclear, the boulder I chose could be reached only by a five foot leap across a deep chasm. It was also a very mossy boulder, and not at all level. First I tried a dry run without the precious camera bag. No problem – the trial went without a hitch. And the more difficult reverse jump, despite a higher landing, was equally successful. Reassured, I picked up the cameras, inadvertently stood in a pool of water, and casually repeated the leap onto my boulder; this time making a fine three-point landing on two elbows and a coccyx. Wiping the tears away, I began setting up the camera. This was done with meticulous care: there would be no retakes on *this* shot. Ten seconds on the timer. Ready, steady, *go!* What I had failed to realise was that being crouched down for so long had given me pins and needles in the legs; making the return jump now was like kicking off from a wet cardboard box. I never stood a chance. Forearms and chin slammed down on the mainland leaving both feet pedalling the chasm. The movement that followed would have made a bull seal look good. *Eight, seven six...* Disoriented I first of all ran the wrong way, tripping over the rucsac I was meant to be carrying for authenticity. *Five, four...* Picking up the rucsac, I about-turned and swung it onto my back on the run. *Three, two...* Then it dawned on me that I was supposed to be *walking* up the ridge, not running a fell race. In the last second I was able to restrain my forward lunge just long enough to hear the faint *click* before taking a header into a gorse bush. Taking pictures? Nothing to it.

An icy wind droned across the summit rocks, freezing my hands to the trig point where I stood oblivious to the cold and gasping at the view. Snowdon, Glyders, Carneddau: an array of fine peaks spread across

Llyn Edno, just below the summit of Moel Meirch (Route D1)

the horizon, each one snow capped as if for ease of iden-
tification. A runner came by – Sue Walsh up from Plas y
Brenin I guessed – and there was a brief moment of visual
discord: I, ponderous in anorak and breeches; she, vital
in vest and shorts. She did not see me, I think, and was
gone in seconds.

Going westwards down the grass ridge was deliciously simple. Probably just as well, because my eyes
were riveted throughout on what must be the best of all
views of Snowdon. Having now begun to think of this
Moelwyns business as being all very straightforward – all
neat little paths and stiles and close-cut grass – it was all
the more startling, not ten minutes later, to find myself
thrashing up a craggy slope by hanging onto clumps of
heather. I had gone the wrong way of course, and the fact
that I knew precisely where and why only made matters
worse. Rediscovering the path on the far side of Carnedd
y Cribiau amounted to being confronted with unassailable evidence of my own stupidity. And it hurts. From
then on I stuck to the path like gob.

I was in a trance. Mesmerised by the hypnotic swing
of boots, the day began to pass for me in the stupor that
must be the saving of shipwrecked sailors and prisoners
in solitary. I felt I had no purpose other than to allow the
day to proceed from dawn until dusk with a minimum of
interference and upset. Llyn Edno came and went in a
hazy recollection of sun sparkles on its miniature ice
flows; while Cnicht was seen in a dream, its decapitated
summit bobbing on an ocean of grass like a ship without
a sail.

The sleepwalk ended at Allt Fawr. I was at the lip of
the great abyss, and in that abyss was Blaenau Ffestiniog
– the kind of town that gets slag heaps a bad name.
Looking back, Moel Siabod now seemed an astonishing
distance away. I couldn't quite believe that only a few
hours before I had scrambled up its east ridge. Then the
evening began laying down little strips of night on the
eastern slopes and it was time to go down.

My arrival at the Crimea coincided with that of a car.
It was driven by a vicar. Confident of early salvation, I
stuck out my thumb and smiled a righteous smile. He

looked the other way and drove past. Instead it was to be the very next traveller, a slick sales rep driving a slick motor, who lifted me out of the gutter and got me safely down to Dolwyddelan. The moral to this story, of course, is that vicars have an acute sense of history.

A pleasant alternative ridge to the summit of Moel Siabod.

VARIANT (A): ASCENT FROM CAPEL CURIG

Distance/Time:
Slightly shorter in distance and time.

Terrain:
Good tracks, grass paths, then a final rock section.

Main Summer Difficulties:
None.

Winter Conditions:
No additional problems.

Special Problems:
Added transport complications in returning from Dolwyddelan.

Start:
Pont Cyfyng, on south side of bridge (734571). Adequate parking.

Finish:
Summit of Moel Siabod.

ROUTE DESCRIPTION

Follow the steep, winding road (surfaced but private) to Rhos Farm. Pass through the farmyard and continue along the track to its end at the far side of an almost level moorland area. Now bear right to begin climbing the north-east ridge by a series of ribs and grass runnels to a narrow, rockier crest. The summit lies at the far end of this to the south-west.

There is also an alternative approach to Daear Ddu starting from Pont Cyfyng. Follow this variant as far as the end of the track, then go left through an area of old quarry workings to reach Llyn y Foel. Continue as for the normal route to the summit of Moel Siabod.

D2: MOELWYNS: SOUTHERN RIDGES

A contrived but
varied and enjoyable
route joining the
three principal
summits of the
southern Moelwyns.

Distance/Time:
15km (9½ miles). 5 hours.

Ascent:
1000m (3300ft)

Major Summits:
Cnicht – 690m (2265ft)
Moelwyn Mawr – 770m (2527ft)
(Moel yr Hydd – 648m (2127ft))
Moelwyn Bach – 711m (2334ft)

Terrain:
Mainly grass with a few rocky sections. Some boggy
ground.

Main Summer Difficulties:
A short easy scramble near the summit of Cnicht.
Occasional rock steps between Moelwyn Mawr and
Moelwyn Bach.

Winter Conditions:
Very variable and not to be underestimated. Some of the
steep grass and shale slopes can be lethal when frozen.
Danger from mine shafts.

Emergency Alternatives:
Descent into Cwm Croesor from Bwlch y Rhosydd
(665463). Descent west from Bwlch Stwlan (661441) to
avoid Moelwyn Bach.

Special Problems:
Route-finding in mist between Cnicht and Moelwyn Mawr.

Approach:
Along A4085 between Beddgelert and Penrhyndeudraeth.
Turn off to Croesor 300m north of Garreg Llanfrothen
(614421).

Start:
Car park at Croesor village (631447).

Finish:
As above.

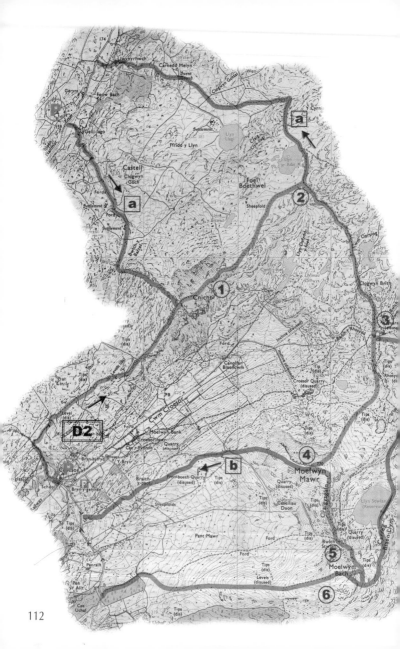

ROUTE DESCRIPTION

Take the steep uphill road out of the village (marked: *No Through Road*) to a gate and stile. Follow a stony track up through woods to where it levels. Fork right and follow a good path – until a stile comes into view on the right skyline. Go over this, then follow the ridge over another stile on the right to a rockier section. Continue up the ridge to a small grass plateau where the Nanmor path arrives. Good scrambling on the right side of the ridge leads to the summit of Cnicht[1] (1½ hours).

Continue along the summit ridge, passing over or around subsidiary tops, and descend a shallow ridge to a cairn overlooking Llyn yr Adar.[2] Turn right and follow a mainly good path, with several short descents, to Bwlch y Rhosydd.[3] Continue straight ahead, passing between old quarry buildings and up an incline, to the upper, boggy plateau. Infrequent marker stones denote the path, until a shallow ridge marked by quartz outcroppings appears on the right. Follow this ridge up a featureless cone to the summit trig point of Moelwyn Mawr[4] (1¾ hours).

Go a short distance east from the summit to locate the connecting ridge to Moelwyn Bach. Follow this over a rocky summit (Craig Ysgafn) and down to Bwlch Stwlan.[5] The easiest way now bears up left along a diagonal scree path until the grassy east ridge is gained and followed up to the summit of Moelwyn Bach[6] (¾ hr).

Descend due west from the summit by a long and gentle grass ridge to the lower pastures. These are crossed by a good path to arrive on a surfaced lane. Follow the lane rightwards into Croesor in 1½ km (1 hr).

By coming upon the Moelwyns a little later in life (hopefully not *too* late!) you will bring to them a maturity of outlook not available in youth; so that you will have more time, more patience, for what are really only very modest hills. You will be able to enjoy

113

Moelwyn Bach from Moelwyn Mawr

them simply for what they are, and not just for what they might have been. Isolated and recognised, it is an outlook that can be usefully applied at other times, to other hills.

The day begins at Croesor, a sleepy backwater with a main street so narrow you'd have to put a cat out sideways. This is the place to start the most interesting ascent of Cnicht – by its south-west ridge. The ridge develops gradually, one stage at a time. First of all there is a leafy lane, a romantic spot but for its 1:2 gradient; then an open, grassy shoulder; and finally a scramble on bare rock to finish. The summit proves not to be the sharp point promised from a distance (with a stretch of imagination, or local pride, Cnicht has been likened to the Matterhorn), but instead an elongated ridge crest peaked with one main summit and numerous subsidiaries. Some people are disappointed by the discovery, which is a little odd when you consider that much of the interest in mountaineering comes from finding things to be different from what they seemed.

To the north, now, stretches that great upland expanse – the backbone of the Moelwyns culminating in the noble head (or ignoble rump, depending on your choice of alignment) that is Moel Siabod. But this day is

going to be more subtle than that. Our path swings around the head of Cwm Croesor instead, passing among the forlorn moorland pools in its descent to the desolated metropolis of Bwlch y Rhosydd.

Ascending the south-west ridge of Cnight at the start of Route D2

Many years have elapsed since the Rhosydd quarry was last worked; and yet on some occasions you can still sense a throb of activity through the ghostly presence of its workforce – men emerging from the lodging houses or mounting the inclines to begin another day of work. A little more each year the spoil settles, iron fittings corrode, grass encroaches; but each year, too, those echoes from the past strengthen in clarity to compensate the loss – a process like the rotting down of flesh on a fallen fruit to release the growing stone.

Already it has taken root. You can see it from a view-point not an hour's walk away across the moor: there, down in the eastern cwm of Moelwyn Mawr – the Stwlan storage dam. Instead of carving up the mountains, this new generation drowns them. No echoes here: the work-force of *this* industry are the tireless turbines housed in the pumping station far below – one of the few efficien-cies in a system of growth which continually fails to sustain its supposed beneficiaries now bewildered and drawing dole in Blaenau Ffestiniog. In the old days of the quarries it paid the manager to keep their workforces in the dark about economics; and in that respect, little has changed. It is thanks to innovations like the Stwlan dam that, as proof of progress, there is now electricity in every home; but it takes more than a flick of a switch before people will see the light.

I wish the climb up Moelwyn Mawr could be more distracting. Under the present mood, its unrelenting slope of steep grass reinforces thoughts of toil and drudgery and unfair treatment. *Why are you doing this to me?* But hammering your fists against its thick skull of compacted

Simple scrambling on the upper part of Cnicht's south-west ridge (Route D2)

116

shale has no more effect than the tickling of an inquisitive ant on a dead elephant's hide. You can hardly expect an answer.

Somewhere in mountain literature there ought to be an essay entitled 'The View From Moelwyn Mawr'. There isn't one, as far as I know; but if there was then I imagine it would have been written by Showell Styles, a writer who has the knack of persuading unwanted mountains like this out of feeling sorry for themselves. For all this, I guess his essay would have been retrospective, even introverted, as it rotated through its 360 degrees and reflected from the metaphorical mirror that surrounds this hill and is responsible for its unrivalled panorama. Quarries, towns, mountains, seas: that is the view. Is that also the ascending order of purity? I sometimes think so; and wonder, on occasions, if the sea might offer me more. Not that I am dissatisfied with my mountains; only that they, and me among them, are feeling just a little bit vulnerable nowadays.

The traverse between the two Moelwyn summits restores those more down-to-earth feelings about mountains and mountaineering. Perhaps this is because the connecting ridge is that much narrower and more involved than might be expected from two such gentle domes; and, if a west wind happens to be forcing grey clouds through the gaps, then its appearance can become quite sinister. In practice there are no sustained difficulties, and the broad col of Bwlch Stwlan is reached without problem. Ahead is Moelwyn Bach – the final summit of the day. *Now* there is a problem. It is one of choice. The first option is to go up soily scree to below the commanding nose of rock which bars access to the summit (and gives the familiar 'face' of some distant profiles), and then to dodge it rightwards over treacherous shelves. That route is too lumpy. Secondly, there is the direct scramble up the left side of the nose on lichenous rock. That is too hard. Finally, beetling its way up left to avoid the nose, is a scree path leading to a grass slope. And that route – like baby bear's porridge – is just right.

The summit area of Moelwyn Bach is surprisingly

Above: *Looking across to Moelwyn Mawr from the summit of Cnicht (Route D2)*

Below: *Final ascent to Moelwyn Mawr on Route D2. In the background can be seen much of Route D1, from Moel Siabod (centre) to Allt Fawr (centre right)*

Above: *The view back to Cnicht from Moelwyn Mawr (Route D2)*

Below: *Moelwyn Bach (right) seen from the descent of its western ridge on Route D2*

broad and flat. Of course there will be a summit cairn somewhere if you can be bothered to go and look for it; but it hardly seems relevant. Descent is down a delightful sweeping ridge of short grass that is as gentle on the feet as it is on the landscape. The view is gentle too: of the Glaslyn estuary and Tremadog Bay; and perhaps even of a sun, somewhere dipping, calling an end to this and everyone else's day.

A much shorter route which nevertheless makes the best of Cnicht.

VARIANT (A):
CNICHT FROM NANMOR

Distance/Time:
9km (5½ miles). 3½ hours. (500m – 1650ft – of ascent)

Terrain:
Mainly good paths, but with a few rocky sections and some boggy ground.

Main Summer Difficulties:
Scrambling on the lower ridge plus the scramble to the summit itself.

Winter Conditions:
No problems in addition to those already mentioned.

Start:
Lane to Gelli Iago on Nanmor road (632484). Adequate parking.

Finish:
As above.

Route Description

Take the track to Gelli Iago, turning off at a footbridge to follow a winding path up Cwm Gelli Iago, keeping to the west bank of its stream. Steep at first, the path eases where it enters the upper cwm. Near the head of the cwm, curve right to a shallow col, Bwlch y Battel – below a blunt ridge. Follow this ridge – steep, rocky, and frequently vague – to emerge on the delightful grass plateau of the south-west ridge normal route. Follow this route, up its short scramble on the right of the ridge, to the summit of Cnicht.

Continue as for the normal route – along the summit

route and down to a cairn overlooking Llyn yr Adar – but then turn left to descend to the east shore of the lake. Follow the path between small outcrops; and then descend a steep slope – first right and then left – to pass below Llyn Llagi. Follow the path across marshland and then down through pastures back to the surfaced lane. Follow this leftwards back to the start in less than 1km.

VARIANT (B): INCORPORATING MOEL YR HYDD AND THE STWLAN DAM

Distance/Time:
No longer but slightly more time consuming than the original.

Terrain:
As for normal route.

Main Summer Difficulties:
Easy scrambling on north-east ridge of Moelwyn Bach.

Winter Conditions:
Not recommended – numerous problems in ascending Moelwyn Bach.

Special Problems:
Locating correct descent to dam. Detailed route-finding when ascending Moelwyn Bach, and on its descent.

Start:
Bwlch y Rhosydd (665463).

Finish:
Croesor.

An interesting, if perverse, series of variations on the main route.

ROUTE DESCRIPTION

Instead of following the incline, go up to a grass shoulder on the left to follow a vague shoulder to the rounded summit of Moel yr Hydd. Descend west, above a line of cliffs, to a level area and junction of paths. If you can find it, a path now goes south, descending gradually, to the north end of the dam wall. Cross the dam, go left through a gate, down steps, and over a low wall on the right. Now work up left to reach and follow a steep ridge to where it levels out below a blunt shoulder. Ascend very steep grass on the right of a quarried cave, continuing up

The Llyn Stwlan dam and Moelwyn Bach (Route D2(b))

a runnel below pumice-like slabs. On reaching the crest (small cairn), turn right and follow the shallow ridge to the summit of Moelwyn Bach.

Reverse the ascent route to the first grass col you encounter, and descend cautiously north down a grass slope to find the path down diagonally left (facing out) over scree to Bwlch Stwlan. Follow the ridge as for normal route in reverse to the summit of Moelwyn Mawr. Descend its excellent west ridge – vague in the lower section – to a surfaced road. Turn right to reach Croesor in a few hundred metres.

E: THE NANTLLE AREA

These are the dispossessed hills of Snowdonia. They have far too much grass, and not nearly enough altitude. They are a little too far south, and very definitely too far west. They attract adjectives like *gentle* and *forgotten,* which endear them greatly to enthusiasts of the obscure, but not to the mainliners whose habit demands a regular dose of Glyder. In the north, their shapely heads dip gracefully into green valleys and supply backdrops for the pretty villages of Beddgelert and Rhyd Ddu; whereas in the south, their ungainly tails fan out coastwards to be nibbled away by industry and other unkind processes.

For all its shortcomings, the area has some excellent rock climbing. Cwm Silyn has an unexpected mountain crag in Craig yr Ogof, with its long climbs of every difficulty. Only its distance from the main centres prevents it becoming more popular. Other mountain crags are less idyllic. They tend to be loose, vegetated, or – not infrequently – both. Unaccountably, one crag is the complete

A cloud sea pours into Cwm Silyn (Route E1)

Nantlle Ridge; summit area of Trum y Ddysgl

antithesis of this description: climbing the compact, barren walls of Castell Cidwm is like scaling the side of a ship without the barnacles. Being more tolerant (oblivious?) of their surroundings, rock climbers also make better use of the coastal region. The Tremadog cliffs, being all of five minutes walk from the café at their foot, attract a tremendous number of climbers onto their tropical walls. The rock here is universally admired, and some of these climbs are among the very best in Wales.

Only occasionally will winter impart its true characteristics. Hardly has the snow fallen before a warm wash of coastal air clears it away. Walking may be snowy, but rarely wintery. Winter climbing is handicapped to an even greater degree, the likelihood of these hills receiving the required number of successive frosts being quite small.

If the picture of Nantlle presented here seems less than ecstatic, it is only to prevent its proper appreciation being swamped by greater expectations. The area has qualities peculiar to itself, and to make mere comparisons of size and ruggedness with other regions would be to undervalue its special charm. The delicate balance of its presentation would be upset; and nothing induces impotence quite so effectively as the pressure to perform.

125

On the Nantlle Ridge; Mynydd Drws y Coed in the background

A short traverse of well-maintained interest across a series of small but shapely hills.

E1: NANTLLE:
THE NANTLLE RIDGE

Distance/Time:
12km (7½ miles). 4 hours. (21km (13 miles) and 6½ hours for the double traverse.)

Ascent:
875m (2900ft)/1200m (4000ft)

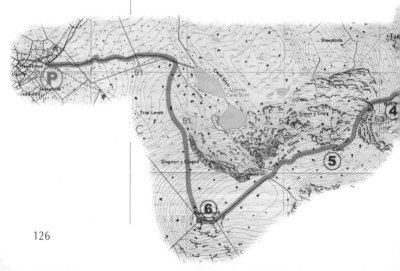

Major Summits:
Y Garn – 634m (2080ft)
Mynydd Drws y Coed – 695m (2281ft)
Trum y Ddysgl – 710m (2329ft)
Mynydd Tal y Mignedd – 655m (2148ft)
Craig Cwm Silyn – 734m (2408ft)
Garnedd Goch – 701m (2301ft)

Terrain:
Varies from grass paths to bare rock. Some boggy ground.

Main Summer Difficulties:
Short scrambles at infrequent intervals along ridge, particularly on Craig Cwm Silyn.

Approach:
Along A4085 between Beddgelert and Caernarfon.

Start:
Car park at Rhyd Ddu (569528).

Finish:
Roadhead at 504512 (careful parking in field by gate), or as above.

ROUTE DESCRIPTION

A popular solution to the transport problem, provided two cars are available, is to begin the traverse at Rhyd Ddu having left one car at the far end. Alternatively, the ridge is not too long as to rule out a double crossing.

From the car park, cross the road and stile to follow a marked path through fields to where it joins the Nantlle Valley road at a 90° bend. Turn left and follow a boggy path over fields.[1] A less distinct path – usually marked *Ridge* – then bears off right to ascend a steep grass shoulder to the summit of Y Garn[2] (1½ hrs).

Y Garn, the first objective of Route E1, seen from Rhyd Ddu

Follow the narrow ridge south then west – some scrambling but all well marked – over Mynydd Drws y Coed and Trum y Ddysgl to the tall obelisk on Mynydd Tal y Mignedd[3] (1 hr).

Continue south-west along the broad grass ridge to descend a steep and badly eroded path into the extended col of Bwlch Dros Bern.[4] The path ahead, ascending the rocks on the north-east ridge of Craig Cwm Silyn, is not obvious at first. It can be tempting to skirt difficulties on the right; but this should be avoided. Instead, start up the rocks just right of the actual crest. Difficulties soon ease, and a good path is gained winding up to the summit area of flat stones[5] (½ hr).

The ridge remains broad and featureless as it passes above Craig yr Ogof towards Garnedd Goch, the final summit of the traverse.[6] The long, gentle shoulder descending northwards leads to a good track which is followed leftwards to the roadhead (¾ hr).

Strange, those different ways of recalling memories of favourite walks. Some are stored in strict chronological order like the sequences of a home movie – *Now this is*

where we started, that's what we did, and this must be where we finished – and no less tedious to project. Others, arranged in little groups, may be accessed randomly like pages of snap-shots in a photo album: *Here's where we stopped for lunch... And isn't that Noel chasing his rucsac down the scree slope?... Yes, and here's the sheep eating Noel's sandwiches while Noel is chasing...* One triggers the next until eventually you get so practised at flicking through the pages and reading out the captions that you aren't remembering the day at all only its pictures. Just now and again, though, you get to keep memories of piercing authenticity. Sight, smell, mood – a complete slice of time captured intact, able to be recalled later as a feelie holograph capable of withstanding the closest scrutiny. You are walking around with the essence of a day in your head, perfectly preserved like a pickled octopus: fish the thing out, and even years after the event and you will still be able to make novel observations. I have memories of the Nantlle Ridge stored in all these different ways.

Cluttering up the 'photo album' are memories of climbing days spent on Craig yr Ogof, long before I ever

From Y Garn, Route E1 continues over Mynydd Drws y Coed

129

On the ascent of Mynydd Drws y Coed (Route E1)

Looking back along the connecting ridge between Mynydd Drws
y Coed and Trum y Ddysgl (Route E1)

thought to walk the ridge: a hot day in the bilberry season
when we stuffed ourselves with the things before frying
to a crisp on the Crucible wall; an afternoon in late
autumn when the air was so still you could inhale the
earth-rich scent of a Gauloise cigarette being smoked a
hundred feet below; a winter day when we crept out of
our Tremadog hibernation for a premature return to the
mountains, only to become petrified gargoyles on the
Ogof Nose; and that blue spring morning when we fought
the Jabberwocky while a cloud sea broke endlessly over
our cliff like the Californian surf.

Good days: good memories. But only one of them
has qualified for the total recall category. It was a day
when I emerged alone from a cliff sizzling in a 30° heat
wave and refused to go down again. There had been a
cooling breeze up there in the evening when I had
strolled over to the summit of Craig Cwm Silyn, and the
hill was completely empty of people. What a waste. In a
great surge of rebellion (because rock climbers are
normally very conservative) I had set off northwards to
rediscover the Nantlle Ridge in the few hours of daylight
that remained.

The col between Trum y Ddysgl and Tal y Mignedd (Route E1)

Unfettered by heavy boots or sac, I had first scrambled down the ridge to a broad col overlooking the head of Cwm Pennant. New Lands. It was there that any lingering sense of obligation to the cliff and climbing was finally absolved. I would go on. Pumping up the soily, eroded slope at the far side of the col, I was met by a lone ridge walker coming the other way. I stood to one side to let him through. We exchanged a glance, a few words – no more – and he passed on, posing for a few moments on a promontory, at my request, for a photograph. The only person I would meet.

The great obelisk of Mynydd Tal y Mignedd came into view on the far side of a grass plateau, casting an ominously long shadow in the low, raking sunlight. There would be no time to climb it today. Must keep moving: carefully across the neck of ridge to Trum y Ddysgl; impatiently above the unique grass cliff of Mynydd Drws y Coed; recklessly over the stones towards Y Garn.

From that outpost I could see all the northern hills. Never before had I witnessed such clarity in the atmosphere. Snowdon, Glyders, Carneddau: each range laid out like the coloured strips of montage, entirely without

Looking back along much of the Nantlle Ridge from Craig Cwm Silyn (Route E1)

the fading colour or detail of aerial perspective. Ireland could be seen quite easily as a bumpy line on the horizon, while the nearer coastline of Anglesey was presented in such meticulous detail that every bay from Caernarfon to Holy Island could be identified. In the Menai Straits, ten miles away, I could see the reflection of a tree.

It was during the return crossing of the ridge, some-where on Trum y Ddysgl, that I saw the hawk. It was hovering a hundred feet above the slope, curious about some tiny movement in the grass. Behind was that unrepeatable view of the Anglesey coastline. I had the memory; now I wanted the photograph. The hawk began circling me as I made ready. There was just one frame left in the camera. It was late, the sun rapidly sinking towards the sea; but I would wait. Sooner or later the hawk would surely pass across that view again. It began stalking me, making low passes like a seagull protecting its eggs. I took to hiding behind rocks, so it would forget about me and resume its search for food; but always it would find me, circling above and peering down on me with its sharp eyes. Sometimes it would glide towards the very place I had planned for it, only to fall out of the sky onto some imaginary shrew as I was about the press the shutter. At other times it would be just a little too high or low, and of course there was only that one frame. So I waited some more, and naturally it got darker on us both.

Now the hawk was doing what it was doing only because that's what hawks do, much as I tried to invest it with malicious intent. But when finally it flew off into the distance, without a sign of ever coming back, I was still both angry and devastated. I'd risked benightment for this one shot, and now the thing had deserted me. Bloody selfish bird.

But I would *not* give up. I began to run up and down the ridge, flapping my arms and making what I guessed might be – God forgive me – hawk-like noises, hoping it would return:

> *Young above an old cliff, weaving*
> *Sense from a cold wind, wearing*
> *Flap coat of crow wings, cawing*
> *Circles in the night...*

... And return it did! It circled once, made a single pass across the pre-arranged space, and then flew off into the sunset. I had my photograph. Twenty minutes later the sun slid under the water like a punctured beachball. And half an hour after that, somewhere on the unfamiliar boulder slopes below Craig Fawr, it was night. The rest I do not care to remember.

F: THE RHINOGS

You could drive around the entire perimeter of the Rhinogs without ever seeing a hill you'd consider worth lacing up your boots for. It's that kind of place. Driving down the east side of the range you come first to Trawsfyndd power station, an unsuitable cube isolated in a fog of unease. Rising beyond the far bank of its steamy lake are the first low hills; an old ridge pressed down into the earth until hardly more than a hump remains, a bone or two protruding at the crest where the skin is stretched tightest.

Further along this road – here as discreet as a Roman nose – there is an unrestricted view of three main peaks: Rhinog Fawr, Rhinog Fach, Y Llethr. But what an uninspiring sight it is; grass on grass, the distant humps of little hills. Hump, hump, hump. Then the road nose-dives into the depths of a no-see-um forest. And very soon the Rhinogs will be quite forgotten.

The southern leg of this circumnavigation is along

Rhinog Fach rising above Llyn Hywel

the shore of the Mawddach estuary. So fascinating is this mountainous scenery, and so narrow and tortuous the road, that the opportunities of self-annihilation during the six-mile drive are limitless. Barmouth, at the southern tip of the tour, completes the degeneration because the hills behind (oh yes, the Rhinogs) are mere diving boards for an imagination now hopelessly besotted by the Atlantic Ocean.

Driving north, on the west side, the situations are neither coastal nor mountainous. Distant surf: distant hills. Instead the road busies itself with pastures and pretty little villages; until eventually what looks to be a giant mud pie comes into view and we find ourselves at Harlech – a town and a castle seemingly tumbling from their uncertain perch on the hillside.

So much for the exterior: so much for the deception.

(Continued on following page)

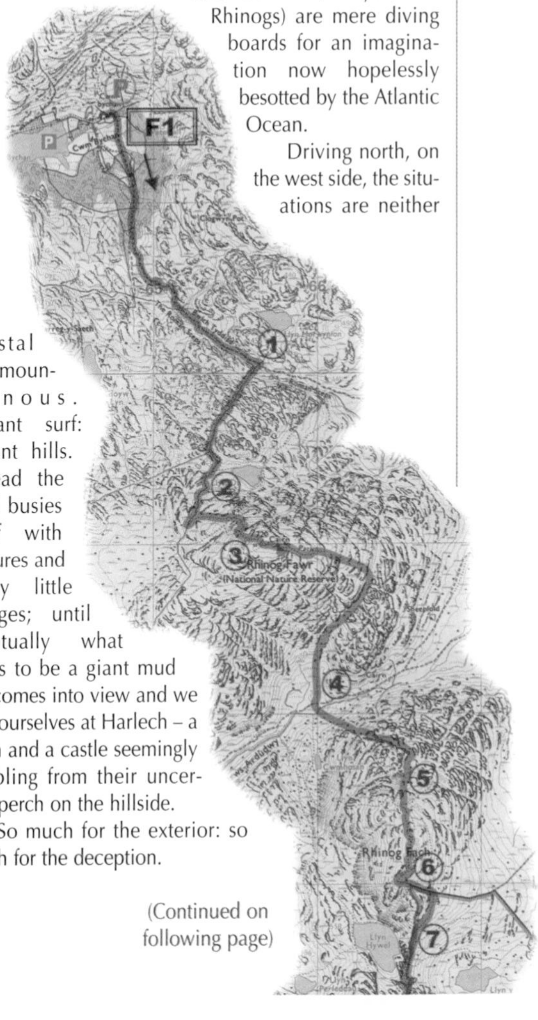

137

A long and tiring
traverse over the main
Rhinog Peaks.

F1: RHINOGS: MAIN TRAVERSE

Distance/Time:
24km (15 miles). 8 hours.
(Add 9km (5½ miles) and 2
hours if a start is made from
Llanbedr.)

Ascent:
1500m (5000ft)

Major Summits:
Rhinog Fawr – 720m (2362ft)
Rhinog Fach – 711m (2333ft)
Y Llethr – 754m (2475ft)
Diffwys – 750m (2462ft)

Terrain:
Rough paths
through heather and boul-
ders, followed by grass paths.

Main Summer Difficulties:
Short, easy scrambles on the Rhinogs. Length.

Special Problems:
Choosing correct line of ascent and descent on
Rhinog Fawr.

Approach:
Along A496 between Llanbedr and Harlech. Follow the
minor road to Cwm Bychan.

Finish:
Barmouth.

(Continued on
following page)

Route Description

Follow the signs to Roman Steps and go along them to
Bwlch Tyddiad.[1] From a little way beyond the actual col,

find a way up right – along a rough path – onto the slopes of Rhinog Fawr. A small pool is passed; then a lake (Llyn Du),[2] beyond which the path begins to rise by a stone wall, later zig-zagging up to the summit and trig point[3] (2 hrs).

Do not attempt to descend directly to Bwlch Drws Ardudwy, but first go east along a spur before bearing right to descend a bouldery path to the col.[4] (The path down right from here leads to Cwm Nantcol and can be used to shorten the traverse.) Continue straight ahead by an appallingly steep and direct path in poor condition. Where it eases, follow a path left then right – up zig-zags – to a cairn and viewpoint overlooking the bwlch.[5] The summit is further south[6] (1½ hrs).

(Continued from previous page)

Again avoid the temptation to descend directly, and first go east to find a path descending near a stone wall to reach rock slabs above Llyn Hywel.[7] Continue by a path near the wall; but then break off right, up steep grass, to the broad summit area of Y Llethr[8] (1 hr).

A wall now runs along almost the entire crest of the remainder of the ridge, making route-finding quite simple. If visibility is poor, however, care is needed to negotiate correctly the westward dogleg beyond Diffwys.[9] Care is also required in crossing the transverse walls and fences that appear with increasing frequency. At the final col of Bwlch y Llan[10] (623176), it is best to quit the ridge leftwards (east) to follow a path by the side of a transmitting station to reach a minor road at 628176,[11] about ½ hr from Barmouth. It is also possible to descend west from the Bwlch, but this is much less simple (3½ hrs).

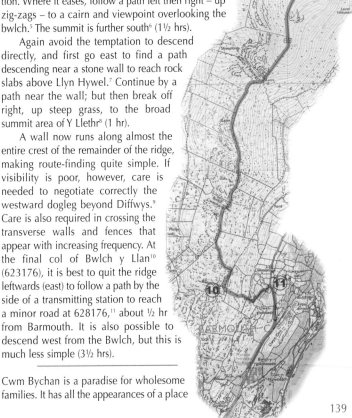

Cwm Bychan is a paradise for wholesome families. It has all the appearances of a place

*The Rhinogs (Route
F1) seen from west.
From left to right:
Rhinog Fawr, Rhinog
Fach, Y Llethr*

with plenty to do without there being actually anything *to* do, which makes for excellent Sunday relaxation. Expensive and energetic dogs are everywhere, prancing up and down the narrow lane in search of timid children to molest. Meanwhile, their owners are settling down for lunch in the leafy shade of the river bank – at wooden picnic tables that have sprung up from the loam like giant toadstools. Permanently damp and spattered with bird droppings, these structures complete the misery of grand-mothers brought here under protest by their country-clad – if not country-born – offspring.

'*Roman Steps*' says the sign at the road end beyond Llyn Cwm Bychan. Steps, yes: Roman, no. But intriguing all the same. This is the mediaeval equivalent of a yellow-brick road: it entices innocents towards the interior, winding a safe passage through the notorious Rhinog heather that is reputed to be the deepest, most tenacious, most chasm-concealing heather in the world. How one would go about the business of verifying that claim I can't imagine; but it is a claim which is rigorously defended by anyone who has so much as *heard* of a Rhinog, let alone made a positive sighting. Anyway, and even though

it applies only to one part of the region, the terrain has
been described thus so often that – as with the Steps –
the description is now held to be an unassailable truth,
whatever the evidence.

At Llyn Du during the
ascent of Rhinog Fawr
(Route F1)

Having been guided with such efficiency to Bwlch
Tyddiad – a deep col on the main ridge – then it is all the
more demoralising to be abandoned to Rhinog Fawr with
no more indication of a route than the ineffectual scuff-
ings of a few would-be pioneers. By the time you have
reached what you dearly hope to be Llyn Du, you are
much more susceptible to all those stories you've heard
about the intractability of the Rhinogs. Being an old
scoffer myself – and having once sat on some miserable
little lump in this vicinity for fully five minutes erro-
neously believing it to be the summit – you will have my
every sympathy.

Once on the real summit, any self-indulgent feelings
of elation are quickly smothered by the worry of having
to find a way down again. Now the trouble with round
mountains – and Rhinog Fawr is *very* round – is that one
slope looks very much like another; and choosing a way
down is like stacking all your roulette chips on one

The descent from Rhinog Fach to Llyn Hywel (Route F1)

number. And if you think about it, those are not the best odds in the world. Which is just what *I* was thinking as I began lowering my feet down yet another miniature crag high above the safe defile of Bwlch Drws Ardudwy. I took consolation in being on the right side of the mountain.

One of the great attractions of mountain walking is having a legitimate excuse (usually exhaustion) for sitting around in remote places for long periods of time and doing absolutely nothing. There is no better place for indulging this than at Bwlch Drws Ardudwy. Sitting on an island of rock, amid a listless sea of heather, with views to east and west, facing an uncompromising grind out of the gap to Rhinog Fach, and with a rucsacful of lunch at your feet, there is every incentive to stay precisely where you are for the remainder of the afternoon. But conscience stirs: rests must be earned, and the ridge is so little done…

Whoever designed the path up Rhinog Fach from here must need his head examined. So must all those who blindly follow. It's like crawling up a coal chute on a Monday morning, if Monday morning is when your coalman happens to call. There is a theory which

The walled ridge of Crib y Rhiw leading to Diffwys on Route F1

On the final section of the Rhinog Ridge (Route F1) as it dips towards Barmouth

proposes that the pleasure of success is directly proportional to the effort expended in its achievement. Rhinog Fach and its north slope support this theory admirably: a short, sharp shock, followed by a right, royal relief. This summit is a good place to be, and for the first time you have some idea of what is happening: Rhinog Fawr, the great rough dome, has fallen behind; Drws Ardudwy, the arch tempter, lies below; and now *this* is the real beginning.

Llyn Hywel fills the next gap. It is an unlikely lake, as precariously held as a full tumbler of whisky in a trembling hand. The ridge here is unusually narrow, cut away above the lake in thin slices of rock slabs; a stone wall further defines the boundary between east and west. The haul up to Y Llethr, the high point of the ridge, is hardly less demanding than that to reach Rhinog Fach; and yet it seems so much less gruelling now that total commitment has been pledged to the enterprise.

The sudden change in character is astonishing. Where once was only heather and boulders is now turf and fine stones. Smooth grass domes have never before seemed so appealing. Not that the ridge has grown dull;

far from it, for the very next section – Crib y Rhiw – is the most ridge-like of all. Along its crest runs a stubborn stone wall, as determined as the Great Wall of China – to which it bears a remarkable resemblance – in going where it was clearly meant to go.

At Diffwys, where the ridge begins a long dogleg westwards, other changes are taking place. The now familiar ridge-crest wall continues as before, but here it is met at regular intervals by transverse walls and fences. Because there has been little loss of altitude to justify this change to pastureland, there is a surreal sensation of walking over ordinary lowland fields that have somehow been lifted up into the sky. Perhaps this is where the sheep have their heaven. As a mere human, of course, you remain solidly down on earth, where the walls and fences have lost none of their tangibility; and whereas most of them are equipped with stiles, you need a certain amount of guile to find and negotiate the more obscure varieties among them. The sheep, naturally, merely spirit their way through.

Enjoyment of my first stroll down this end of the ridge was marred by a slight problem with visibility I was having at the time. It was pitch dark. What is more, it had been like that for two hours and showed all the usual signs of remaining that way for a good bit longer. But what could I do? Problems like that don't just go away of their own accord. Not even if you wish and wish and thump the ground in a small private tantrum. I know: I tried. No, they have to be lived through, *won* through – just like wars and plagues and *The Sound of Music*.

Night time induces unrepresentative behaviour, so I'll skip the rest of the story about how I tried to find a way down into Barmouth through ten acres of brambles, over a back garden fence, and through a noisy front gate onto the high street wearing a black balaclava and carrying a bag over my shoulders. Besides, I've been through it all before at the police station.

G: CADER IDRIS

Cader Idris defines the southern limit of Snowdonia's mountains. High ground continues southwards, beyond the park boundary, but each successive line of pine-cloaked hills in that direction is increasingly mountainous. The name Cader Idris, though commonly used to identify the highest point (Pen y Gadair), and literally 'The chair of Idris', meaning the horseshoe ridge around Cwm Cau, is applied to a whole string of summits arranged in the line of a long ridge – the characteristic shape so frequently seen at the southern limit of visibility from the peaks of central Snowdonia.

Not surprisingly, in view of its rugged terrain, the mountain has a big potential for rock climbing. Encumbered by a history of spasmodic exploration, however, the area has been slow to claim its rightful place in Welsh climbing, and this despite two major mountain crags – Craig y Cau and Cyrfrwy – and a number of low-lying outcrops. Winter potential is similarly inhibited. Once again, the obvious challenges are on Cau and Cyfrwy; although the big vegetated crags below Pen y Gadair and Mynydd Moel – hardly worth a second glance in summer – come into their own during these conditions.

The best ridge walk here might be expected to follow the main ridge from east to west; but that would be to exclude the fine ridge which curls around Cwm Cau towards the summit of Pen y Gadair. In practice a compromise can be struck up to include the best of both: a circuit of Cau elongated to include Cyfrwy and Mynydd Moel.

Though often maligned for its overpopularity, the mountain of Cader Idris is nonetheless fascinating. Because apart from providing extensive views of surrounding hills, it has unique scenic qualities of its own. There is also a legend: a night spent alone on Pen Y Gadair, it is said, will make you a poet or a madman.

G1: CADER IDRIS:
CIRCUIT OF CWM CAU

A circular ridge walk visiting or viewing the most interesting features of Cader Idris.

Distance/Time:
13km (8 miles). 4½ hours.

Ascent:
950m (3100ft)

Major Summits:
Mynydd Pencoed – 798m (2617ft)
Pen y Gadair – 893m (2928ft)
Mynydd Moel – 855m (2805ft)

Terrain:
Good paths almost throughout. Some rock, and one section of boggy ground.

Main Summer Difficulties:
Short scrambles of minimal difficulty on Mynydd Pencoed and Pen y Gadair.

Special Problems:
Route-finding in bad visibility between Pen y Gadair, Mynydd Moel, and the broad descent ridge.

Approach:
Along the A487 between Dolgellau and Machynlleth.

Start:
At the Idris Gates (733115), 100m along the B4405 from the road junction at Minfford. Limited parking opposite the gates, so it is best to park at the large car park near the road junction.

Finish:
As above.

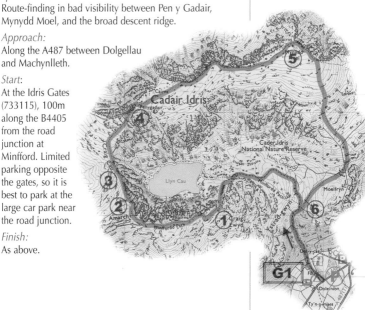

Llyn Cau and Mynydd Pencoed (Route G1)

ROUTE DESCRIPTION

Walk down the Abergynolwyn for a few hundred metres to the Idris Gates. Go through the gate entrance, along a once fine avenue of trees, and cross a footbridge. Beyond a gate, the stony path zig-zags steeply up through woods to emerge at a more level section. Continue along the main path, circling into Cwm Cau. At a large cairn, follow a rough path steeply up left to gain the crest of the ridge which encloses the cwm.[1] Follow the ridge, keeping near the crest, as it circles the cwm towards the summit of Mynydd Pencoed. There are fine views of Llyn Cau and the big cliffs of Craig y Cau above it. Just before reaching the summit, there is also an impressive view down the Great Gully, with Pencoed Pillar on its right (looking out)[2] (1¾ hrs).

Continue around the head of the cwm, dropping steeply to a col.[3] About half-way up the subsequent rise to Pen y Gadair, contour left to arrive on the Pony Track, where there is a fine view of the Cyfrwy Arête and beyond towards the Rhinogs and even Snowdon. The summit is soon reached by following the Pony Track up an easy scramble. There is a shelter 30m north of the trig point[4] (1¾ hrs).

Llyn Cau (Route G1)

The view south towards Mid Wales from the ascent to Mynydd Pencoed (Route G1)

Descend north-east over rocky ground to a level section; and then continue near the north edge, over a subsidiary top, to the shelter circle at the summit of Mynydd Moel[5] (¾ hr).

Continue east a little way from the summit, over a stile, before trending south-east then south down a broad grass shoulder. By keeping close to the fence running down the steepening shoulder, and using stiles to cross and recross, follow a vague path – improving in the lower region – until it leads through a break in the wall to rejoin the approach path just above a pine plantation.[6] Follow this main path down left to the Idris Gates (1¾ hrs).

At Minffordd, while peering through the Idris Gate, I saw a boychild running through an avenue of trees, his long hair writhing in the wind like serpent tails. The sound of the wind and the sound of his voice was one and the same thing: a controlled, mournful wail. It was as if he was fleeing from his own angry threat. On the trunk of each tree in the avenue, mouths began to appear – creamy yellow splits, cracking and spitting; while above them, dark notched eyes blinked open beneath a film of sticky sap. One by one the trees uprooted themselves and rose unsteadily onto their spindle feet, shaking their leaves at the little boy who ran past them, faster and faster, down the avenue. But the noise of the wind rose above the wailing and shaking; until even the trees themselves cowered before it, wrapping themselves up in their branches to fend off the screeching sound. The little boy had now reached the far end and was safe. But he did not stop: instead he ran and ran, his lungs burning, until he was high up on the mountainside. Meanwhile the wind gusted harder and harder and the trees bent lower and lower; until, one by one, they blew over, thudding into the path like falling giants, the breath of life bursting out of them in a gush of stale air.

In time the wind subsided, leaving the dead trees in dirty piles across the floor. Cautiously I stepped over them, wondering what would happen if one were not quite dead. And then I too was on the open mountainside.

Circling the rim of Cwm Cau from Mynydd Pencoed to Pen y Gadair (Route G1)

'*And where do you think you are going at your age?*'

Startled – I had though myself alone – I spun around to face the challenger. But no-one was there. Everything was just as before: the woods of Cwm Rhwyddfor below, a stream cascading into their shade; the solitary sheep grazing meagre clumps of grass among the heather; and the zig-zag path along which, not five minutes before, I had emerged into the full sun of the morning… *The path – somehow I had inadvertently left it to cross this stream.* I hurried back across to regain it and continue into the cwm.

Seeing into the cwm, a sight previously denied from any viewpoint, was like being allowed to share in some fiercely kept secret: something rare and intimate and female. Though unsure of what I was meant to do with the knowledge, I stared and stared so I would not forget.

'*Hey! Look who's down there!*'

There was nowhere to hide. High above the lake, on the tip of Mynydd Pencoed, stood a group of jeering figures; tiny specks at this distance, half familiar, half recognised, but without names or faces.

'*Yeah, we saw you looking!*'

I began to run, breathless up the stone flank of the ridge; anything to get away from the soft belly of the cwm, away from the guilt. I looked across again, but the figures had gone. Would they tell? Below was Llyn y Cau, rippling and laughing and covering herself up. I'd been framed.

This side of Cader was a new experience for me; and being alone with it meant again having to live through that awkward adolescent mixture of romance and debauchery. Having outgrown the sense of childlike wonder (at the fallen avenue of trees), and as yet unable to sustain maturity of outlook (at the summit), all that was left to me was lust: lust for the misty, *contre jour* veils drawn over Corris; lust for the fatty rib of Pencoed Pillar; and lust for the moist walled cleft of Great Gully. Captivated by the novelty of what was happening, I was – like most first-timers – incapable of fully embracing the essential nature of my experiences.

Fires were burning on the rough grazing land above Dolgellau. The blue smoke rolled listlessly into the valley, feeding a sluggish river of chimney smoke already making its way towards the coast. Emphasised by that diffuse

The Cyfrwy Arete seen in profile from Pen y Gadair (Route G1)

background, the needle-sharp outline of Cyfrwy Arête rose out of its cwm, Llyn y Gadair dark at its foot like a prick of black blood. There was more to this mountain than could be comprehended by egotistical youth: I grew older to accommodate the new experiences. By the time I reached the summit I was well into middle age.

Forced away from the summit by the approach of a group of real people, I took off in the direction of the Fox's Path in order to relive a moment from an earlier adventure. It had been late winter then, the mountain top covered in plates of ice, and my gully barely hidden under its thin ribbon of old snow. It shouldn't have been so difficult to find; and yet though I searched the cliff with my memory of it I could locate not a single matching feature. Maybe it never happened. Maybe I wasn't caught by darkness. Maybe I never spent that night alone on the summit. Who knows, when this mountain is so full of illusions?

Time began to contract. A mile flowed underfoot without the surfacing of a single thought by which to catalogue its passage. Mynydd Moel came and went like a profitless meeting with a stranger; and the whole of the

View back along the ridge to Pen y Gadair from Mynydd Moel (Route G1)

descent towards the woods passed without a flicker of significance. Even a hazy view into Cwm Cau stirred no youthful memories. Suddenly weary, I paused by a stream above the woods to ease the rucsac straps from my shoulders and to rub away some of the stiffness in my legs.

'And where do you think you are going at your age?'

I looked up, already knowing no-one would be there. I was sitting on the very same rock where I'd heard the voice before. But there were differences: now my skin was wrinkled and my hair turned white; and now, having come full circle, I was as old as the hills.

An interminable agony of jarring bones accompanied my zig-zag descent through the woods. Time had expanded again; so that each painful moment had to be lived through, relieved only by the sure knowledge of an eventual end to it all – the inner contentment of the dying. The fallen trees of the avenue no longer held for me any fear or fascination; I stumbled over them with arthritic clumsiness. By now my skin had turned a purple grey; and even as I walked it began dripping away from the bones in bloody lumps, so that by the time I reached the Idris Gate there was nothing left. Strength gone, my skeleton clung feebly to the bars of the closed gate, rattling and screaming a torment of imprisonment. So violent was the shaking and rocking that my unsupported skull toppled from its neck and plopped through the bars, rolling into the middle of the B4405. It was seen there by a small boy who dribbled it all the way down to Abergynolwyn to show his dad, who was tending his begonias at the time and not much interested. My soul, meanwhile, was driving away unnoticed in the opposite direction, madness intact and anticipating an early tea.

H: THE ARANS

The region south of Bala has never attracted mountain walkers in great numbers. Isolated from the rest of Snowdonia, it continues to suffer a disproportionate neglect. The Aran Ridge is responsible for most of what little traffic there is; and this has the effect of introducing an unnatural concentration of outsiders into an otherwise quiet farming region. As with Nantlle's ridge (there are many similarities between the two), the Aran Ridge has been the focus of a protracted access wrangle – in this case only recently, and as yet partially, resolved. Ironically, confrontations between farmers and walkers have publicised the area to such a degree that it has become more, not less, popular than before.

Rock climbing, though less troubled, is equally handicapped by isolation. The cliffs of Cwm Cywarch are the best known; and, being spared the access difficulties now suffered by their counterparts on the northern section of the ridge, are likely to remain so. Meanwhile, climbers

Summit of Aran Fawddwy

heading for those sensitive areas – towards Gist Ddu for instance – must continue to tread softly and hope no-one notices or cares.

Don't expect too much of the Arans. They can justify only a few superlatives, so it would be a pity to have those devalued by an unwarranted and aimless splash of praise. They are what they are, and that's quite good enough.

H1: THE ARANS: MAIN TRAVERSE

Distance/Time:
15km (9½ miles). 5 hours.

Ascent:
800m (2600ft)

Major Summits:
Aran Benllyn – 884m (2901ft)
Aran Fawddwy – 907m (2971ft)

Terrain:
Mostly good paths over grass, some rock. Boggy on alternative descent.

Main Summer Difficulties:
None.

Special Problems:
Care is required on both descents in bad visibility: to the west, in negotiating a featureless slope; and to the east, in guarding against an unexpected drop on the south flank of Drws Bach.

Approach:
Along the A494 between Bala and Dolgellau. From Llanuwchllyn, follow the B4403 for 1km.

Start:
Layby at 880297. Adequate parking.

A pleasant, undemanding ridge walk over the main Aran summits.

Finish:

Cwm Cywarch (852188); or on minor road near Esgair Gawr (816227).

ROUTE DESCRIPTION

Go over the stile at the layby to follow a well-signed path: first along a track, then rightwards over pasture, and finally onto the start of the

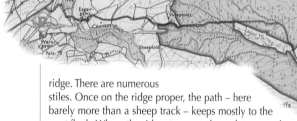

ridge. There are numerous stiles. Once on the ridge proper, the path – here barely more than a sheep track – keeps mostly to the west flank. Where the ridge steepens, the path turns rocky and ascends nearer the crest. It steepens again – passing a subsidiary summit – to the summit of Aran Benllyn[1] (2½ hrs).

The way ahead to Aran Fawddwy is obvious and incurs little height loss. A final steepening leads to its rocky summit and trig point[2] (1 hr).

Go along the vague ridge top to a cairned subsidiary summit,[3] and continue beyond it to a junction of fences. There are two stiles; take the one on the left for Cwm Cywarch (a); and the one on the right for Esgair Gawr (b).

(a) Turn left after crossing the left-hand stile, following a rough path near a fence, down Drws Bach and onto a level grass ridge and good path.[4] Follow the ridge onto a plateau area beyond the head of Hengwm[5] (approximately to a point on the map marked as a spot height 568). From here, a path goes diagonally down the south-east flank of Hengwm into Cwm Cywarch (1½ hrs).

Or (b) After taking the right-hand stile, go down a very vague ridge of rock and grass, heading almost due west towards a narrow break in the forestry trees (a break also taken by the Afon Harnog). The path is marked in

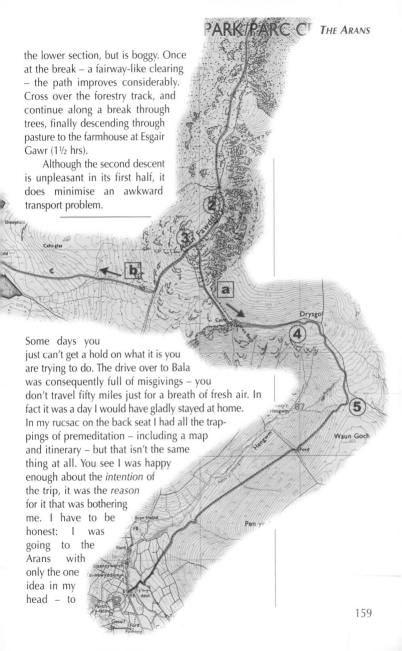

the lower section, but is boggy. Once at the break – a fairway-like clearing – the path improves considerably. Cross over the forestry track, and continue along a break through trees, finally descending through pasture to the farmhouse at Esgair Gawr (1½ hrs).

Although the second descent is unpleasant in its first half, it does minimise an awkward transport problem.

Some days you just can't get a hold on what it is you are trying to do. The drive over to Bala was consequently full of misgivings – you don't travel fifty miles just for a breath of fresh air. In fact it was a day I would have gladly stayed at home. In my rucsac on the back seat I had all the trappings of premeditation – including a map and itinerary – but that isn't the same thing at all. You see I was happy enough about the *intention* of the trip, it was the *reason* for it that was bothering me. I have to be honest: I was going to the Arans with only the one idea in my head – to

159

Aran Fawddwy from Aran Benllyn (Route H1)

'tick' the ridge. So now you know what had stuck in my throat.

Bala was pulled taut into a state of pre-season tension: its shops overflowing with merchandise, yet empty of people. It must be a difficult time. Poncing around in my breeches, looking to buy lunch, I felt uncomfortably like the first butterfly of summer.

I pulled over in a layby down near the lake to make an early reconnaissance of the ridge. At that point the hills were still many miles away; but such was the depth of my reluctance that I was willing to be dissuaded as soon as possible. In the event the ridge looked welcoming; not challenging – that would have turned me away – just ordinarily good. And that was fine by me, because doing something just because it 'looked good' didn't demand any complicated justifications.

The walk itself began less convincingly. Leaving the car a little way beyond Llanuwchllyn, at a parking bay I considered insufficiently removed from ordinary people and ordinary life (always a bad start), I felt as though I was dropping-out without conviction or dignity. A National Park access sign pinned to the first stile added to the discomfort: *If you must run away from your responsibilities and besmirch this beautiful landscape with your grubby little feet, then the least you can do is to walk where people can easily clean up after you: KEEP TO THE PATH...* or words to that effect. You don't just feel small, you feel round as well – like a sheep dropping.

While we're at it, do you want to know why climbers avoid answering the question: *Why do you climb?* Why instead they narrow their eyes as if to answer by staring at some distant and imaginary peak? I'll tell you: they are unable to answer because they haven't got an answer to give; and they haven't got it because they daren't ask themselves for one. Oh, there's one hiding deep inside them alright, waiting to come out; but it never will because they won't let it. Not that this is wholly surprising. Suppose, for instance, you asked a boxer what compels him to box; however true it may be, you could hardly expect the answer: *Because I like to see the other bloke's eyes wobble when I hit him.* Could you? Well:

Aran Benllyn from Drws Bach (Route H1)

neither can you expect a climber (or walker or mountaineer – they're all the same) to tell you that they continue to go up mountains because they've never grown out of it. It would be self-incriminating. So that 'distant stare' of the mountaineer isn't an unspoken explanation, it's an identity crisis.

I took the question of my own identity crisis up Aran Benllyn to see if something couldn't be done about it. It could: I forgot the question. Conveniently *at one* with the mountains again (i.e. fantasizing as normal), I celebrated my recovery by drooling at an unremarkable view eastwards from the summit. Precisely because it was nothing special to look at – like an attractive but unmasterly painting – it was that much more available for being incorporated into the fantasy. The view took on a universal significance. Now perhaps it had something to do with the uninterrupted roll of the hills; or the way the light was falling; or maybe even the relativity of the configuration – impassive object, impassioned observer. But either way, seeing as whatever it was had this 'universal significance', it made justification for being there as unnecessary as justification for being alive. At which point you realise they are one and the same thing.

Looking back across the head of Hengwm during the descent of Aran Fawddwy
(Route H1)

Footbridge in Cwm Cywarch (Route H1)

A discovery not without its significance.

Not that everything had been roses. On my way up to Benllyn I had hoped to catch a glimpse of Gist Ddu, a fine crag above Llyn Lliwbran on which I had climbed some years previously. But the negotiated path in this region studiously avoids all the interesting places; in fact – and be warned – it is deadly boring. It was only when nearing the summit, having realised that I had missed the crag completely, that I had begun to enjoy the situations and views for what they were. Had I seen the crag, I suspect I may well have forsaken the ridge for a day on its wonderful rough rock. Some people have no sense of purpose.

Halfway towards Aran Fawddwy I felt I wouldn't have wanted it any other way. Because now there was the great feeling of being utterly involved with the terrain; of being adrift in a rough sea of heather and rock. Not *starting* or *finishing*, with all those silly little ideas and emotions that such periods seem to generate; but *middling*, which for me is what ridge walking is all about. It has something to do with being able to remain at altitude without all that tedious business of sitting about at summits, trying to prolong a supposed moment of exhilaration with a series of empty ejaculations.

Having undergone all this tiresome analysis, it will come as no surprise if I say that I arrived at the end of the ridge in a state of absolute confusion. Not only was I uncertain of why I had done it, but I wasn't even sure of what it was I'd done. Fearing insanity (*fearing* insanity?), I was relieved to see other people out and about and looking suspiciously as if they too might be contemplating the traverse. And if enough people do a thing then it makes it okay – right?

I got a lift back to my car with some kind fellow who insisted on giving me the talk about proper careers and family responsibilities (hitch-hikers will know what I mean). Honestly, you'd think he was talking to someone who didn't know where he was going.

I: SNOWDONIA TRAVERSES

As far as many people are concerned, the idea of contriving a traverse over a number of hill ranges – of extending a route beyond its natural dimensions by crossing a road to connect it with another ridge system – is going completely against the grain of the ridge walking ethic. Besides, there is more than a hint of competitiveness in the concept; or, at the very least, a mode switch away from hill walking and into the realm of upland travel.

In practice there is less to argue about. One of the more satisfying aspects of ridge walking – and this quite apart from any qualities of position or outlook – lies in the outright challenge of a long and arduous route. For most people, the preceding routes in this book will adequately supply that need, especially in imperfect weather. And yet there will be occasions when your arrival at a peak of fitness coincides with an abnormally high level of motivation and you will want to do more. What then? An extended traverse could be the answer.

The obvious plan of joining up a couple of ridge walks that happen to lie on adjacent ranges is somehow unsatisfactory. Instead, the best trips seem to grow from the core of a linking idea, however contrived that might at first appear. South–north traverses (or vice versa) have that sense of purpose. Beginning at Barmouth, for instance, it would be quite possible to design a traverse over the Rhinogs, Moelwyns, and Carneddau, finishing at Aber after about four days of splendidly remote ridge walking. Circular tours fulfil a similar purpose, and have the advantage of easing transport problems. As an example, the Moelwyns, Hebog/Nantlle group, Snowdon, Glyders, and Carneddau can be logically connected in this way. Finally, there is the idea of connecting summits which happen to rise above a given altitude. This may seem the least satisfactory excuse of all; and so it would be were it not for the coincidentally superb traverse of the fourteen peaks whose summits lie above 3000ft. This, the most famous of all extended ridge traverses in Snowdonia, is quite rightly the subject of this chapter.

I1: SNOWDONIA TRAVERSES: THE FOURTEEN PEAKS

Summary:
An exceptionally long and tiring traverse over three main hill ranges, linking the fourteen highest peaks of Snowdonia.

Distance/Time:
60km (37 miles). 16 hours.

Approaching Great Pinnacle Gap on Bristly Ridge (Route I1)

Carnedd Llewelyn (centre left), Yr Elen (right) and Carnedd Dafydd (rear) seen from the ridge near Foel Fras (Route 11)

Ascent:
4000m (13200ft)

Major Summits:

Foel Fras – 942m (3091ft)
Foel Grach – 974m (3196ft)
Carnedd Llwelyn – 1064m (3485ft)
Yr Elen – 961m (3152ft)
Carnedd Dafydd – 1044m (3423ft)
Pen yr Ole Wen – 979m (3211ft)
Tryfan – 917m (3010ft)
Glyder Fach – 994m (3262ft)
Glyder Fawr – 999m (3279ft)
Y Garn – 946m (3104ft)
Elidir Fawr – 942m (3030ft)
Crib Goch – 921m (3022ft)
Crib y Ddysgl – 1065m (3495ft)
Snowdon – 1085m (3559ft)

Terrain:
Everything from soft grass to bare rock ridges.

Main Summer Difficulties:
Numerous scrambles spread throughout the traverse. Length.

Special Problems:
Logistics.

Approach:
Along A55 between Bangor and Conwy to Aber village.

Start:
At Aber, or road end at 676716. Adequate parking.

Finish:
Pont Bethania (627506) on A498 between Beddgelert and Pen y Gwryd. It is not normally possible to use public transport to return to Aber.

ROUTE DESCRIPTION

1)*Carneddau:* Ascend A1 (b), passing over Drum,[1] Foel Fras,[2] and Foel Grach,[3] to Carnedd Llewelyn.[4] Now follow A3 to Yr Elen,[5] retracing the final part back to the col above Llyn Caseg. Make a slightly rising traverse rightwards (WATER), using a faint path, to Bwlch Cyfryw Drum

(683637). Continue as for A2, over Carnedd Dafydd[6] and Pen yr Ole Wen,[7] to Glan Dena[8] (668605) (WATER) (6½ hrs).

2) Glyders: Cross the road, over a stile, and up a scree tongue and gully onto the first shoulder of Tryfan north ridge. Follow B1, over Tryfan[9] and up Bristly Ridge, to Glyder Fach.[10] Use B1 (c), via Glyder Fawr,[11] to get to Llyn y Cŵn[12] (WATER), and B1 (d) to Y Garn.[13] Descend to the next col and contour the hillside on a good path curving left to gain and follow a ridge up to Elidir Fawr.[14] Descend vague paths on the south slope – scree then grass – to reach good paths and tracks (WATER) leading down into Nant Peris[15] (607587) (5 hrs).

3) Snowdon: Go east up road to Blaen y Nant[16] (623570). Turn right, over bridge, and follow path up towards Cwm Glas Mawr. Cross the stream and head towards a cleft in the hillside up on left marked on map as 'Fall' (622562) (WATER). Scramble up left side of fall onto Crib Goch north ridge. Follow C1 (a) Crib Goch,[17] then C1, over Crib y Ddysgl,[18] to Snowdon Summit.[19] Descend by C2 to Bwlch Cwm Llan[20] (605522), and then by C2 (a) to Pont Bethania (4½ hrs).

Tradition demands that the Fourteen Peaks be traversed in the faster direction of Snowdon to Aber; and this continues to be much the most popular way. However, in the proper context of this book, the southward route offers greater interest. (It may be that your chief interest is to record a fast time, in which case you would do better going northwards; the 'official' traverse – for record purposes – being the fastest time between Snowdon and Foel Fras, taking all

Y Garn (centre), Foel Goch (right) and Elidir Fawr (rear right) seen from near the summit of Tryfan (Route 11)

intermediate summits above 3000ft on the way.) Consider these advantages of a southward traverse.

(1) The most tedious slopes – Pen yr Ole Wen and Elidir Fawr – are taken in descent.

(2) Interesting scrambles such as Tryfan north ridge and Bristly Ridge, normally avoided, can be incorporated into the ascent sections.

(3) Finishing on Snowdon, apart from being aesthetically acceptable, has motivational advantages.

(4) Finding a way down in darkness is easier on Snowdon than on Foel Fras.

Naturally, there are also some disadvantages.

(i) Overall time – for record purposes – will be slower.

(ii) The most difficult terrain – gaining and crossing Crib Goch – comes at the end, when you are least able to cope with it safely.

(iii) The soft grass of the Carneddau, as opposed to the hard tracks of Snowdon, would have been more welcome at the end of the day.

Records apart, note that we are still talking about a one-day traverse. And that means travelling light and fast; it means choosing the right day and the right companion.

These requirements are worth considering in detail.

◇ *Travelling light* means just what it says; this is no time to be throwing in extra bits of gear merely through force of habit. You need to have a reason for including or omitting each item of equipment. To demonstrate this (but without suggesting for a moment that this compromise is what you should take), here is a complete list of what I took on a recent traverse during perfect Easter weather when almost all the snow had melted.

◇ *Lightweight leather boots* – already a known quan-

Crib Goch (left) and Crib y Ddysgl (centre) seen from the descent of Elidir Fawr (Route 11)

tity from shorter walks.

⬦ *Stockings/socks* – combination dictated by need to fill boots correctly.

⬦ *Shorts & tracksuit trouser* – maximum versatility for minimum weight.

⬦ *Thermal T shirt* – dual function for both hot and cold periods.

⬦ *Polycotton jacket* – low weight, maximum versatility and comfort.

Looking back to the Pinnacles of Crib Goch from Crib y Ddysgl (Route 11)

174

- ✧ *Pile pullover, thin gloves, balaclava, sun hat, sunglasses, map, compass* – good insurance for little weight.

- ✧ *Daysac* – with waistbelt for stability.

- ✧ *Headtorch* – not an emergency item except in high summer.

- ✧ *Compact camera* – no time for more elaborate picture taking.

- ✧ *Plastic cup* – avoids gulping of cold stream water i.e. stomach pains.

- ✧ *Sandwiches* – 6 slices, moist fillings.

- ✧ *Fruit* – 3 pieces, for waterless sections.

- ✧ *Sweets/chocolate* – for morale as much as energy.

Even though the list obviously highlights some personal preferences and prejudices, one or two central factors emerge. Note especially that, because of the unusually long time spent at altitude, it is necessary to cater for a wide temperature range. After an afternoon of slogging uphill in blazing sunshine, a late evening breeze over a ridge at 3000ft can feel very cold indeed, especially when you are tired. Note also that even though waterproofs were not taken, an adequate degree of windproofness was assured in the choice of jacket and trousers. The omission of other normal emergency items was equally deliberate and considered.

Travelling fast, in this sense, means being realistic about pace and rest stops. Think of it this way: ten minutes rest on each summit adds up to more than two hours of lost time. Unnecessary rests like this are counterproductive. Instead, wait for occasions when you have to stop anyway – to drink or to check the route. On a trip like this, even walking on the level must be considered restful. High morale is equally important in maintaining

The view east from the summit of Snowdon on Route 11: Moel Siabod (left), Lliwedd (right) and Llyn Llydaw (below)

pace; and the best way of achieving it is to set realistic targets so as to be certain of meeting them.

The *right day* for the Fourteen Peaks – given suitable weather – falls on the day you most want to do it. Because without that there is no way you'll be able to force your legs into doing more than they normally would – and that won't get you *half way* to Snowdon. This is assuming, of course, a state of physical readiness; not that anything exceptional is required, just that which comes from regular long hill walks.

The *right time of the year* falls somewhere between April and September. Outside of that season there are simply too few hours of daylight for comfort. The prospect of a winter traverse is very attractive; but you can almost forget the idea of completing it in one day. Even spreading it out over a weekend, the traverse would need extraordinarily good and consistent snow conditions to make it really worthwhile.

The *right companion* is, as already suggested, perhaps the most elusive requirement of all. Those who already enjoy a good, workable partnership will have no difficulty; but others may find themselves with no alternative but to go it alone. Though hard to justify on safety grounds, this solution can be more acceptable than forging a marriage of convenience between two incompatible people who might then talk each other into pushing too hard, or into giving up too easily. One person alone is sometimes better able to judge a situation dispassionately.

Despite all these and other logistical problems, it is well worth trying to get it together for this unique expedition. It may prove to be the hardest day of your life; but it will be one you'll never forget.

APPENDIX:
PRONUNCIATION AND MEANING OF WELSH WORDS

PRONUNCIATION

In general:
- vowel sounds are *pure* sounds (i.e. sound is constant rather than shaped)
- stress is on penultimate syllable
- spelling is usually phonetic (only one sound for each consonant).

Vowel sounds

Short

a	as in rat
e	as in pen
i	as in pin
o	as in top
u	as in swim
w	as in foot
y	as in rim
y	as in nurse (the word y and yr also uue this sound)

Long

a	as in barb
e	as in dale
i	as in seen
o	as in shore
u	as in bean
w	as in tool
y	as in mean

Consonants

b	
c	as in cap
ch	as in the German nacht
d	
dd	as in the
f	as in of

ff	as in o*ff*
g	as in *g*o
ng	as in si*ng*
h	
l	
ll	a hissed l sound
m	
n	
p	
ph	
r	as in English, but trilled
rh	as in English, but with stronger emission of breath
s	as in *s*it
si	as in *sh*op
t	
th	as in *th*ought

Examples

The following suggested pronunciations are only approximate:

Tryfan	*trur*-van
Crib y Ddysgl	kreeb ur *this*-gl
Moel Cynghorion	moil king-*horr*-eeon
Bwlch y Tri Marchog	bulkh ur tree *marr*-khog

GLOSSARY

aber	river mouth
aderyn (ader)	bird (birds)
afon	river
allt	wooded hill
aran	high place
bach	small, little
blaen	end, point, top, head of
bod	dwelling
bont	bridge
braich	arm, branch
brwynog	place of rushes/reeds
bryn	hill
bwlch	col
cadair	chair
cae	field

capel	chapel
carn/carnedd	cairn/heap
caseg	mare
castell	castle
cau	hollow
cefn	ridge, back
clogwyn	cliff
coch	red
coed	trees, wood
craig	crag
crib	comb (sharp ridge)
cribin	rake (rocky ridge)
cwm	hollow, valley, cirque
cynghorion	counsellors
dau, dwy	two
dinas	fortress, city
dôl	meadow
drws	door
du, ddu	black
dwr	water
dyffryn	valley
esgair	ridge
fach	small, little
fawr	large, big, great
ffordd	road
ffynnon	spring, well
ffridd	enclosed grazing
foel	rounded/bare hill
gallt	wooded hill
garn/garnedd	cairn/heap
glas	blue (green)
goch	red
glyn	valley
gwastad	plane, level
gwyn, gwen	white
gwynt	wind
hafod	summer dwelling
haul	sun
hebog	hawk
hen	old
hendre	winter dwelling
isaf	lower, lowest

llan	church, village
llech	flat stone, slate
llithrig	slippery
lloer	moon
llwybr	path
llwyd	grey
llyn	lake
lôn	lane
maen	stone, block
maes	field, meadow
main	narrow
marchog	horseman
mawr	large, big, great
melyn, melen	yellow
moch	pigs
moel	rounded/bare hill
mynydd	mountain
nant	brook
newydd	new
ogof	cave
pen	head, top
perfedd	middle (entrails)
pont	bridge
pwll	pool
rhaedr	waterfall
rhiw	hill, slope
rhos	moor
rhyd	ford
saethau	arrows
tal	front, end
tri	three
trum	ridge, summit
twll	hole
ty	house
tyddyn	small farm, cottage
uchaf	upper, highest
un	one
wen	white
wrach	witch
y, ŷr	the
yn	in

EMERGENCY CHECKLIST

1: MOUNTAIN RESCUE

INTERNATIONAL DISTRESS SIGNAL:

Six long blasts on whistle (or torch flashes), followed by a one-minute pause. Repeat.

TO ALERT MOUNTAIN RESCUE:

Dial 999 and ask for Police/Mountain Rescue. Have details ready (written if possible) of:
- name and description of injured person
- exact location of injured person (including *Grid Reference* and map *Sheet Number)*
- time and nature of accident
- extent of injuries.

(Also be prepared to give information on weather conditions – cloud base/wind/visibility etc.)

And then remain by the phone until met by Police Officer or member of Mountain Rescue.

GRID REFERENCE:

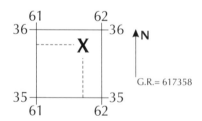

A G.R. is unique only if it is preceded by the map Sheet Number.

RESCUE HELICOPTERS:

(1) Secure all loose equipment before arrival.

(2) Identify position with arms raised in a V as helicopter approaches. *DO NOT WAVE.*

(3) Protect injured person from downdraught.

(4) Allow winchman to land of his own accord.

(5) Do not approach a landed helicopter unless directed by one of the crew.

2: FIRST AID

HYPOTHERMIA (EXPOSURE) VICTIM:

When preventative methods have failed:

(1) Recognise possible signs (some or all of the following: unexpected behaviour, muddled thinking, quietness, stumbling). *Violent shivering* may precede hypothermia; but it is when this stops that hypothermia really begins.

(2) Stop and prevent further heat loss (shelter, insulate).

(3) Supply warmth (food, hot drink, body heat of companions).

(4) Prepare to move if victim's condition has improved (i.e. shows rational behaviour, etc.). If condition has *not* improved, lie victim curled up in a slightly head down attitude.

(5) Descend by quickest and most sheltered route practical (but be prepared to stop again and repeat procedure if victim's condition deteriorates).

(6) Send advance party to alert rescue services if practical.

Remember: Never assume death in an unconscious exposure victim – continue treatment.

FIRST AID ESSENTIALS:

Calm and reassure the patient (and yourself) and then:

(1) *Check breathing and airway:*
- clear airway if necessary
- turn unconscious patients to lie in the *three-quarter-prone* position.

(2) *Check for severe bleeding:*
- stop bleeding by maintaining direct pressure with an improvised pad, and elevate.

(3) *Check for broken bones:*
- do not move patient if fractured spine is suspected
- immobilise other fractures with improvised splints and slings
- keep patient warm and comfortable while waiting for rescue services
- monitor condition.

This is a *checklist*: if you are unsure of how to apply these procedures, then *find out now, before you are called upon to use them*.

NOTES

NOTES

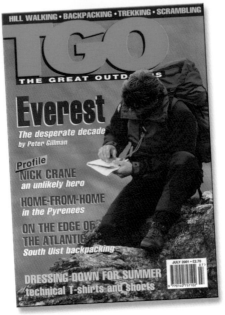

LISTING OF CICERONE GUIDES

NORTHERN ENGLAND
LONG DISTANCE TRAILS
- THE DALES WAY
- THE ISLE OF MAN COASTAL PATH
- THE PENNINE WAY
- THE ALTERNATIVE COAST TO COAST
- NORTHERN COAST-TO-COAST WALK
- THE RELATIVE HILLS OF BRITAIN
- MOUNTAINS ENGLAND & WALES
  VOL 1 WALES
  VOL 2 ENGLAND

CYCLING
- BORDER COUNTRY BIKE ROUTES
- THE CHESHIRE CYCLE WAY
- THE CUMBRIA CYCLE WAY
- THE DANUBE CYCLE WAY
- LANDS END TO JOHN O'GROATS
  CYCLE GUIDE
- ON THE RUFFSTUFF -
  84 BIKE RIDES IN NORTH ENGLAND
- RURAL RIDES NO.1 WEST SURREY
- RURAL RIDES NO.1 EAST SURREY
- SOUTH LAKELAND CYCLE RIDES
- THE WAY OF ST JAMES
  LE PUY TO SANTIAGO - CYCLIST'S

LAKE DISTRICT AND
MORECAMBE BAY
- CONISTON COPPER MINES
- CUMBRIA WAY & ALLERDALE
  RAMBLE
- THE CHRONICLES OF MILNTHORPE
- THE EDEN WAY
- FROM FELL AND FIELD
- KENDAL - A SOCIAL HISTORY
- A LAKE DISTRICT ANGLER'S GUIDE
- LAKELAND TOWNS
- LAKELAND VILLAGES
- LAKELAND PANORAMAS
- THE LOST RESORT?
- SCRAMBLES IN THE LAKE DISTRICT
- MORE SCRAMBLES IN THE
  LAKE DISTRICT
- SHORT WALKS IN LAKELAND
  BOOK 1: SOUTH
  BOOK 2: NORTH
  BOOK 3: WEST
- ROCKY RAMBLER'S WILD WALKS
- RAIN OR SHINE
- ROADS AND TRACKS OF THE
  LAKE DISTRICT
- THE TARNS OF LAKELAND
  VOL 1: WEST
- THE TARNS OF LAKELAND VOL 2:
  EAST
- WALKING ROUND THE LAKES
- WALKS SILVERDALE/ARNSIDE
- WINTER CLIMBS IN LAKE DISTRICT

NORTH-WEST ENGLAND
- WALKING IN CHESHIRE
- FAMILY WALKS IN FOREST OF
  BOWLAND

- WALKING IN THE FOREST OF
  BOWLAND
- LANCASTER CANAL WALKS
- WALKER'S GUIDE TO LANCASTER
  CANAL
- CANAL WALKS VOL 1: NORTH
- WALKS FROM THE LEEDS-
  LIVERPOOL CANAL
- THE RIBBLE WAY
- WALKS IN RIBBLE COUNTRY
- WALKING IN LANCASHIRE
- WALKS ON THE WEST PENNINE
  MOORS
- WALKS IN LANCASHIRE WITCH
  COUNTRY
- HADRIAN'S WALL
  VOL 1 : THE WALL WALK
  VOL 2 : WALL COUNTRY WALKS

NORTH-EAST ENGLAND
- NORTH YORKS MOORS
- THE REIVER'S WAY
- THE TEESDALE WAY
- WALKING IN COUNTY DURHAM
- WALKING IN THE NORTH PENNINES
- WALKING IN NORTHUMBERLAND
- WALKING IN THE WOLDS
- WALKS IN THE NORTH YORK
  MOORS BOOKS 1 AND 2
- WALKS IN THE YORKSHIRE DALES
  BOOKS 1,2 AND 3
- WALKS IN DALES COUNTRY
- WATERFALL WALKS - TEESDALE &
  HIGH PENNINES
- THE YORKSHIRE DALES
- YORKSHIRE DALES ANGLER'S GUIDE

THE PEAK DISTRICT
- STAR FAMILY WALKS PEAK
  DISTRICT/STH YORKS
- HIGH PEAK WALKS
- WEEKEND WALKS IN THE PEAK
  DISTRICT
- WHITE PEAK WALKS
  VOL.1 NORTHERN DALES
  VOL.2 SOUTHERN DALES
- WHITE PEAK WAY
- WALKING IN PEAKLAND
- WALKING IN SHERWOOD FOREST
- WALKING IN STAFFORDSHIRE
- THE VIKING WAY

WALES AND WELSH BORDERS
- ANGLESEY COAST WALKS
- ASCENT OF SNOWDON
- THE BRECON BEACONS
- CLWYD ROCK
- HEREFORD & THE WYE VALLEY
- HILLWALKING IN SNOWDONIA
- HILLWALKING IN WALES VOL.1
- HILLWALKING IN WALES VOL.2
- LLEYN PENINSULA COASTAL PATH
- WALKING OFFA'S DYKE PATH
- THE PEMBROKESHIRE COASTAL
  PATH

- THE RIDGES OF SNOWDONIA
- SARN HELEN
- SCRAMBLES IN SNOWDONIA
- SEVERN WALKS
- THE SHROPSHIRE HILLS
- THE SHROPSHIRE WAY
- SPIRIT PATHS OF WALES
- WALKING DOWN THE WYE
- A WELSH COAST TO COAST WALK
- WELSH WINTER CLIMBS

THE MIDLANDS
- CANAL WALKS VOL 2: MIDLANDS
- THE COTSWOLD WAY
- COTSWOLD WALKS
  BOOK 1: NORTH
  BOOK 2: CENTRAL
  BOOK 3: SOUTH
- THE GRAND UNION CANAL WALK
- HEART OF ENGLAND WALKS
- WALKING IN OXFORDSHIRE
- WALKING IN WARWICKSHIRE
- WALKING IN WORCESTERSHIRE
- WEST MIDLANDS ROCK

SOUTH AND SOUTH-WEST
ENGLAND
- WALKING IN BEDFORDSHIRE
- WALKING IN BUCKINGHAMSHIRE
- CHANNEL ISLAND WALKS
- CORNISH ROCK
- WALKING IN CORNWALL
- WALKING IN THE CHILTERNS
- WALKING ON DARTMOOR
- WALKING IN DEVON
- WALKING IN DORSET
- CANAL WALKS VOL 3: SOUTH
- EXMOOR & THE QUANTOCKS
- THE GREATER RIDGEWAY
- WALKING IN HAMPSHIRE
- THE ISLE OF WIGHT
- THE KENNET & AVON WALK
- THE LEA VALLEY WALK
- LONDON THEME WALKS
- THE NORTH DOWNS WAY
- THE SOUTH DOWNS WAY
- THE ISLES OF SCILLY
- THE SOUTHERN COAST TO COAST
- SOUTH WEST WAY
  VOL.1 MINEH'D TO PENZ.
  VOL.2 PENZ. TO POOLE
- WALKING IN SOMERSET
- WALKING IN SUSSEX
- THE THAMES PATH
- TWO MOORS WAY
- WALKS IN KENT BOOK 1
- WALKS IN KENT BOOK 2
- THE WEALDWAY & VANGUARD WAY

SCOTLAND
- WALKING IN THE ISLE OF ARRAN
- THE BORDER COUNTRY -
  A WALKERS GUIDE
- BORDER COUNTRY CYCLE ROUTES

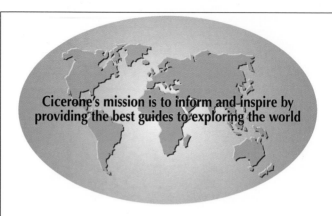

Cicerone's mission is to inform and inspire by
providing the best guides to exploring the world

Since its foundation over 30 years ago, Cicerone has specialised in publishing guidebooks and has built a reputation for quality and reliability. It now publishes nearly 300 guides to the major destinations for outdoor enthusiasts, including Europe, UK and the rest of the world.

Written by leading and committed specialists, Cicerone guides are recognised as the most authoritative. They are full of information, maps and illustrations so that the user can plan and complete a successful and safe trip or expedition – be it a long face climb, a walk over Lakeland fells, an alpine traverse, a Himalayan trek or a ramble in the countryside.

With a thorough introduction to assist planning, clear diagrams, maps and colour photographs to illustrate the terrain and route, and accurate and detailed text, Cicerone guides are designed for ease of use and access to the information.

If the facts on the ground change, or there is any aspect of a guide that you think we can improve, we are always delighted to hear from you.

Cicerone Press
2 Police Square Milnthorpe Cumbria LA7 7PY
Tel:01539 562 069   Fax:01539 563 417
e-mail:info@cicerone.co.uk   web:www.cicerone.co.uk

CICERONE